THE HUTCHINSON ENCYCLOPEDIA

Family

QUIZ

Book 3

THE HUTCHINSON ENCYCLOPEDIA

Family

QUIZ

Book 3

Helicon

Copyright © Helicon Publishing Ltd 1995

Helicon Publishing Ltd
42 Hythe Bridge Street
Oxford OX1 2EP

Printed and bound in Great Britain by
Cox & Wyman Ltd, Reading, Berkshire

ISBN 1-85986-112-1

British Cataloguing in Publication Data
A catalogue record for this book is available
from the British Library

Quiz Numbers

Contributors

Christopher Gray
Antony Moore
Stephen Webster

Editors

Managing Editor
Hilary McGlynn

Project Editor
Bruce Gibbons

Text Editor
Louise Jones

Production
Tony Ballsdon

Page make-up
TechType

EASY

General Knowledge 1

1   In which city is the headquarters of the United Nations?

2   What was the title of the memoirs of former intelligence officer Peter Wright, which Britain tried to ban in 1987?

3   What are the Long Man of Wilmington and the Cerne Abbas Giant?

4   Which 1993 film finally won Steven Spielberg Oscars for Best Film and Best Director?

5   What was the pedestrian equivalent of a highwayman?

6   Whose unsuccessful challenge for the Conservative Party leadership in 1990 brought down Margaret Thatcher?

7   Which public holiday is celebrated in the USA on 4 July every year?

8   What was Michaelangelo's first name?

9   Which media tycoon acquired the *Sun*, the *News of the World*, and *The Times*?

10   In which galaxy do we live?

Answers on page 159

1   Who was hit by a falling apple and so discovered gravity?

2   Who made all things relative?

3   Who placed the Sun at the centre of the solar system?

4   Who first developed the theory of evolution by natural selection?

5   Who turned a telescope on the stars, saw sunspots, and spent his final years under house arrest?

6   Crick was one of the scientists who discovered the structure of DNA. Who was the other?

7   Who gave electrifying lectures at the Royal Institution in the mid-19th century?

8   Who rang a bell – and then collected saliva?

9   Nobel prize-winning physicist Ernest Rutherford was a native of which country?

10   What was Galileo's surname?

Answers on page 159

Africa

1   Which country unilaterally declared independence in
     November 1965?

2   The flag of Libya is a plain rectangle of which colour?

3   Which country was called Upper Volta until 1984?

4   Who was the Egyptian king whose tomb and treasures
     were discovered in the Valley of the Kings in 1922?

5   Who was the Egyptian president who was assassinated
     in 1981?

6   Name the East African country which lies on the
     Equator.

7   Which volcano in Tanzania is the highest mountain in
     Africa?

8   Which explorer did the *New York Herald* send Henry
     Stanley to find in 1871?

9   What are the two main arms of the River Nile called?

10   Which country, bordering Zaire, takes its name from
     the former name of the Zaïre river?

Answers on page 159

Science Miscellany

1 Which scientific unit gives a measure of loudness?

2 Which animals are arthropods and have eight legs?

3 What name is given to an atomic particle carrying a negative charge?

4 Which is the modern scientific unit of work and energy?

5 The behaviour of sound in rooms and concert halls is a separate science. What is its name?

6 Chlorine, fluorine and bromine belong to which family of elements?

7 DNA is found in which part of the cell?

8 What name is given to the change of state from liquid to gas?

9 What kind of an animal is an iguana?

10 Which scientist first said that the Earth rotates around the sun?

Answers on page 159

Colours 5

1 What part of a redshank is red?

2 What is the better-known name for quicksilver?

3 Which grain crop comes in white, red, brown and black varieties?

4 What colour is the central strip on the French flag?

5 Who does Alice follow down a hole into Wonderland?

6 Who made the albums *The Dark Side of the Moon* and *The Wall*?

7 Who composed the waltz *The Blue Danube*?

8 Which pop group provided the voices for the cartoon *Yellow Submarine*?

9 Which canal joins the Red Sea and the Mediterranean?

10 Of which country was Greenland a colony until 1981?

Answers on page 159

Senses 6

1   Which part of the eye contains light-sensitive cells?

2   Which composer wrote much of his finest music when he was deaf?

3   Which nerve carries information from the eye to the brain?

4   How do bats 'see in the dark'?

5   Which part of the eye gives it colour?

6   Which part of the eye gets smaller when the lights go on?

7   What name is given to the colour-sensitive sense cells in the eye?

8   What phenomenon is characterized by constant sound in the ears?

9   How many basic tastes can the human tongue distinguish?

10   Which bones pass sound waves through to the interior part of the human ear?

Answers on page 159

Water, Water, Everywhere 7

1   What is the chemical symbol for water?

2   What is the better known name for the fatal disease hydrophobia whose sufferers have convulsions at the sight of water?

3   Which is the world's largest ocean?

4   Who wrote the *Water Music*?

5   Why are fluoride salts added to some drinking water?

6   Which star sign depicts a man pouring water from a jar?

7   Which president was toppled by the Watergate scandal?

8   Complete the title of Charles Kingsley's classic novel *The Water-*...

9   What is the name for small rivers which join a major one along its length?

10   Which mythological figure fell in love with his own reflection in a pool?

Answers on page 160

Kings and Queens

8

1 How many Kings of England have been named George?

2 Of which dynasty was Elizabeth I the last monarch?

3 Who became king of Spain on General Franco's death?

4 Which king of England was killed while hunting in the New Forest?

5 In which century did Cleopatra live?

6 What was the nickname of Louis XIV of France?

7 Who was Elizabeth I's mother?

8 Which country deposed King Constantine II in 1967?

9 Which English king defeated the French at Agincourt?

10 Which Shakespearean king gave shares of his kingdom to two of his daughters, but not to a third?

Answers on page 160

10

Time 9

1   How many seconds are there in an hour?

2   Which device uses the Sun to tell the time?

3   Which crystal keeps time inside today's mass-produced watches?

4   What type of clocks are the most accurate timekeepers?

5   How many electronic pips does the British Broadcasting Corporation broadcast on the hour?

6   From a building in which London borough are all time zones calculated?

7   Who wrote *The Time Machine*?

8   Which device is used to keep time in music?

9   What is the main scientific time unit from which all others are calculated?

10   Where was the first known public clock located?

Answers on page 160

1 Who was *Singin' in the Rain* in 1952?

2 Who was backed by the Shadows?

3 Which group's hits include 'Surfin' USA' and 'Good Vibrations'?

4 Which singer and songwriter had a successful partnership with Art Garfunkel?

5 Which destructive English rock band made the rock operas *Tommy* and *Quadrophenia*?

6 Which bandleader disappeared on a flight from England to France in 1944?

7 Which soul singer had a posthumous hit with '(Sittin' on the) Dock of the Bay'?

8 Who sang about *1999* in 1982?

9 Which singer became a star in *Funny Girl*?

10 Which band started their notorious career with 'Anarchy in the UK'?

Answers on page 160

1   Which instrument does James Galway play?

2   What is the name of the variation of lawn tennis played by children on a smaller court?

3   Which creature has species called white, tiger, hammerhead and basking?

4   'Cerebral' refers to which part of the body?

5   The failure of which crop caused famine in Ireland in 1845?

6   Who wrote the science-fiction novel *Brave New World*?

7   Which group of people belong to Equity?

8   Who lives at number 11 Downing Street?

9   Who is the patron saint of travellers?

10   On which inland sea do Russia and Turkey have shores?

Answers on page 160

Animal Kingdom

1   What name is given to animals that eat both flesh and plant material?

2   How long is a giraffe's neck, approximately?

3   Why do fish have gills?

4   What kind of an animal is a marmoset?

5   Which animal can run at 110 kph/70 mph?

6   What is the favourite food of the giant panda?

7   What is the name given to the study of birds?

8   What is the fastest animal on two legs?

9   Which animal can move by jet propulsion?

10   What kind of an animal is a gecko?

Answers on page 160

1   What was the former name of Iran?

2   Which country is the world's largest producer of tea?

3   What is the capital of Pakistan?

4   With what is the Japanese art of bonsai concerned?

5   Which 13th-century Mongol warlord controlled probably a larger area than anyone in history, from the Yellow Sea to the Black Sea?

6   Where did the Gang of Four try to seize power in 1976?

7   Which native East Asian plant is the richest natural vegetable food?

8   The West Bank of which river has been occupied by Israel since 1967?

9   Which Asian island is the second largest island in the world?

10   What colour is the circle on the Japanese flag?

Answers on page 161

Human Body

1   What is the scapula?

2   What is the scientific name for the kneecap?

3   Which part of the brain regulates physiological
       stability in the body?

4   Which is the most acidic part of the digestive system?

5   What is protected by the cranium?

6   Which organ is responsible for regulating the blood
       sugar level?

7   What is the name of the large muscle just beneath the
       lungs?

8   Which organ makes urine?

9   Where in the body is the thyroid?

10   What is the scientific name for the human 'tail'?

Answers on page 161

Comedians and Clowns   15

1   Who made the film *The Life of Brian*?

2   What was the name of Tony Hancock's radio show?

3   On which television show did Fozzie Bear, Kermit the
     Frog and Miss Piggy first become popular?

4   What was the title of Walt Disney's 1940 feature-
     length 'Silly Symphony'?

5   Which comic pair starred in such films as *The Road to
     Morocco* and *The Road to Singapore*?

6   To which race does the comic character Astérix
     belong?

7   In Jerome K Jerome's book, how many men were in a
     boat?

8   Who starred in the hit comedies *10* and *Arthur*?

9   What was Bugs Bunny's catchphrase?

10   Who is Punch's wife?

Answers on page 161

1   What would you find if you travelled to the centre of the solar system?

2   Which two planets take less time than Earth to orbit the Sun?

3   Which planet is named after the Roman goddess of love?

4   Which planet is named after the sky-god who was father of the Titans?

5   What kind of extraterrestrial object has been named after the 17th-century astronomer Edmond Halley?

6   Which planet has a day which lasts eight months?

7   Visible sunspots vary in number according to a cycle of how many years?

8   What is the term for a natural satellite?

9   Which planet is usually the furthest from the Sun, but sometimes not?

10   How many planets are there in the solar system?

Answers on page 161

1   Who created the mischievous schoolboy hero William?

2   Who wrote *For Whom the Bell Tolls* and *The Old Man and the Sea?*

3   Which great book was started in Bedford Jail in 1675?

4   What animal story was Anna Sewell's only published work?

5   What sort of animals did Richard Adams write about in *Watership Down*?

6   Who hunted Moby-Dick?

7   Complete the title of Shakespeare's play: *The Two Gentlemen of ...*

8   What sort of factory did Roald Dahl write about?

9   How far under the sea were Jules Verne's explorers?

10 Which magic land did C S Lewis write of?

Answers on page 161

1   Which 'unsinkable' ocean liner sank with the loss of
     1,513 lives?

2   Which force is used by maglev transport systems?

3   What is the name of the world's only supersonic
     airliner?

4   Which rocket transported the *Apollo* crews to the
     moon and back again?

5   Human-powered aeroplane *Gossamer Albatross* made
     which crossing in 1979?

6   What is the abbreviated name given to the French
     high-speed trains?

7   Which was the first mass-produced car with four-
     wheel drive?

8   Which ship transported Charles Darwin around the
     biological beauty-spots of the Victorian era?

9   The ancient Greeks went to war with which kind of
     boat?

10   What was the 'Penny Farthing'?

Answers on page 161

1   Which footballer famously wept when he was booked in a World Cup semi-final?

2   What is the style of Japanese wrestling where very large men fight in a circular ring?

3   In lawn tennis, what name is given to a score of 40–40?

4   What is the name of the competition for teams of professional male golfers from the USA and Europe?

5   How many points are scored for a touchdown in American Football?

6   In golf, what is the name of the grassed area between the tee and the green?

7   In which game would you find cover point, silly mid off, and square leg?

8   Who, at the 1984 Olympics, won the 100 m, 200 m, the sprint relay and the long jump?

9   Which sport featured in many of the Beach Boys' earliest hits?

10   Which sport uses asymmetrical bars, rings and a pommel horse?

Answers on page 162

1   What was the nickname of World War I aviator Baron von Richthofen?

2   For what purpose did Melvil Dewey devise his decimal system in 1876?

3   Who was Sherlock Holmes' assistant?

4   Who was Pope for only 33 days in 1978?

5   What are the indigenous people of New Zealand called?

6   Who was the 'King of Rock 'n' Roll'?

7   What term is used for an official count of the population?

8   Which American statesman flew a kite in a thunderstorm to prove that lighning is electricity?

9   Who was the film star who married Prince Rainier III of Monaco?

10   Who introduced the potato and tobacco to Europe?

Answers on page 162

1   Which international sport uses rings and parallel bars?

2   How many players are there in a netball team?

3   Who issues letters called encyclicals?

4   Who wrote the *Brandenburg Concertos*?

5   Who was the first English printer?

6   Who cut off Samson's hair?

7   Which volcano buried Pompeii?

8   What is the name for a triangle with two sides and two angles the same?

9   What nationality is singer Placido Domingo?

10   What is the musical term for a distance of eight notes?

Answers on page 162

1   Which is the most common gas in the atmosphere?

2   What is the Earth's core made of?

3   Which Indian state is at the eastern end of the
     Himalayas?

4   Which fuel is formed by the fossilization of plants?

5   What is the world's deepest ocean?

6   What is the name of the liquid rock which pours from
     a volcano?

7   Oxygen forms approximately what proportion of the
     atmosphere?

8   What is the term applied to the process of gathering
     together weather forecasts from various recording
     stations?

9   What is the correct name for a 'tidal wave'?

10   What kind of natural phenomenon 'meanders'?

Answers on page 162

1   Who was Lord Melbourne, after whom the city of Melbourne is named?

2   Which Australian state has no land borders with any other state?

3   In which year did Melbourne host the Olympic Games?

4   Which famous song did the Australian journalist Banjo Paterson write?

5   Queen Alexandra's birdwing, found on Papua New Guinea, is the world's largest species of what?

6   By what name is the Solomon Sea better known?

7   What is Australia's largest state?

8   Rockhampton in Queensland lies on which geographical line?

9   What was the main purpose of James Cook's first voyage to the South Pacific?

10   In what type of fiction did New Zealand's Dame Ngaio Marsh specialize?

Answers on page 162

1   What type of coal is brown and fibrous?

2   What raw material is used for making glass?

3   Which form of carbon conducts electricity?

4   What is the sticky wax obtained from sheep?

5   What is the strong inelastic material found in a human tendon?

6   What is the name of the strong material found in plant cell walls?

7   What is the trade name for the non-stick material used for coating cooking pans ?

8   What material forms the hard outermost layer of a human tooth?

9   What is the main component of the metal steel?

10   What name is given to the brittle kind of iron used for making engine blocks and manhole covers?

Answers on page 162

1   Which city was the capital of West Germany from 1949 to 1990?

2   Which is the largest of the Balearic Islands?

3   Which river runs through Budapest?

4   Which two countries have a border with Liechtenstein?

5   In which country is Legoland Park?

6   Which European country colonized Brazil?

7   Which French river flows into the sea at St Nazaire and is famous for its chateaux?

8   Which country is divided into cantons?

9   Where is the Tivoli amusement park?

10 From which city did Neville Chamberlain claim that he had brought back 'peace in our time'?

Answers on page 163

1   What part of a car's engine conveys electricity to the spark plugs?

2   Which development in information technology uses light waves to transfer information?.

3   Which electrical device is used to increase or decrease voltage?

4   What name is given to the heavy spinning plate used in some engines to smooth the power output?

5   What is the name of the process by which a patient is given extra blood during an operation?

6   What does FM stand for?

7   In a sound system, which device is used to increase the strength of the signal from the CD player?

8   Which device in a motor car controls the transmission of power from the gear box to the wheels?

9   What name is given to the study of airflow over moving objects?

10   Which process is used to kill bacteria in dairy milk?

Answers on page 163

1   Who was Franklin D Roosevelt's wife, who helped draw up the Declaration of Human Rights in 1945?

2   Who was Stan Laurel's comic partner?

3   Who was Louis XVI's wife, guillotined in 1793?

4   What were the Montgolfier brothers known for?

5   Who was Othello's wife in Shakespeare's play?

6   Which pair make up the constellation Gemini?

7   Who was closely associated with Dr Jekyll in Robert Louis Stevenson's classic novel?

8   According to legend, which two brothers founded Rome?

9   Who was Bertie Wooster's impeccable manservant?

10   Who were the sons of Adam and Eve?

Answers on page 163

Murders and Assassinations 28

1   Who was assassinated in Dallas on 22 November 1963?

2   Which playwright was murdered in a Deptford tavern in 1593?

3   Which country's prime minister was Olof Palme, who was assassinated in 1986?

4   Who murdered at least five women in Whitechapel in 1888, but was never caught?

5   Who had seven members of a rival gang killed on St Valentine's Day 1929?

6   Who wrote *The Murder of Roger Ackroyd*?

7   Which rock singer was shot dead by a fan in 1980?

8   Which Shakespearean character is haunted by the ghost of his murdered father?

9   What method of execution was used during the French Revolution?

10   In which city was Archduke Franz Ferdinand of Austria assassinated in 1914?

Answers on page 163

1   Who preceded Ronald Reagan as American president?

2   In which country did Pol Pot lead the feared Khmer Rouge?

3   Who was Italy's Fascist leader from 1925–43?

4   What is the official residence of the president of France?

5   In which country are the politicians Yitzhak Rabin and Yitzhak Shamir active?

6   Which British political party is also known as the Tory party?

7   Which human-rights organization campaigns for the release of political prisoners worldwide?

8   Who set out his political ideas in *Mein Kampf*?

9   What offence was former Panamanian leader Manuel Noriega tried for in the USA?

10   How often are American presidential elections held?

Answers on page 163

1   Which striking building designed by Jørn Utzon
     stands beneath Sydney Harbour Bridge?

2   Which artist made his name with paintings of soup
     cans and Coca-Cola bottles?

3   Which famous painting by Frans Hals is in the
     Wallace collection in London?

4   Which name, intended as an insult, was used to
     describe the style of Monet and other French painters
     of the 1870s?

5   Who sculpted the figure of *David* now in the
     Accademia in Florence?

6   What did Gutzon Borglum carve into the face of
     Mount Rushmore, South Dakota?

7   In which English resort would you find the oriental-
     style Royal Pavilion?

8   In which century did Rembrandt live?

9   To which English monarch was Hans Holbein court
     painter?

10   Where was Leonardo da Vinci born?

Answers on page 164

1   Who invented the electric light bulb?

2   Which card game, derived from whist, was first played in Britain in 1903?

3   In which war was the Battle of Naseby fought?

4   Of what breed of dogs are King Charles, Sussex and Pekingese varieties?

5   Which animal is the source of cashmere?

6   Which company made the TriStar passenger plane?

7   What is the normal colour of the gem sapphire?

8   What is the popular name for the Central Criminal Court in London?

9   What feature of Cyrano de Bergerac's anatomy added to his fame?

10   Whose first holiday camp opened at Skegness in 1935?

Answers on page 164

1   Which element is given the symbol H?

2   Which element is used as a germicide in swimming pools?

3   Which element is used in the manufacture of computer microprocessors?

4   The purity of which element is measured in carats?

5   Which element is mixed with copper to make brass?

6   Which lightweight metal is used in the manufacture of aircraft, cars and ships?

7   What is another name for lanthanide?

8   Which element was found in Greenland in 1989?

9   Which element is used to treat indigestion and stomach acidity?

10 Which element is used to make the rod found inside an ordinary electric battery?

Answers on page 164

1   On which river are the Niagara Falls?

2   What is the capital city of Canada?

3   Which district in Los Angeles became the centre of the film industry from 1911?

4   Which party did John F Kennedy belong to?

5   Which American state provided the title of a Rodgers and Hammerstein musical in 1943?

6   Who was killed with all his men at the Battle of Little Big Horn in 1876?

7   Which is the world's largest French-speaking city after Paris?

8   What is the city in Nevada known for its gambling casinos and nightclubs?

9   What is the nickname of Alaska?

10   Which president of the USA was elected for four terms of office?

Answers on page 164

1   In a surgical operation which kind of doctor is responsible for putting the patient to sleep?

2   During a transfusion which tissue is given to the patient?

3   What kind of drug prevents the spread of a bacterial infection through the body?

4   When was hormone-replacement therapy first used?

5   Too much of which type of beverage can cause high blood cholesterol levels?

6   Which type of fat is recommended for healthy eating?

7   A new pacemaker will assist which organ?

8   Someone with gastroenteritis is having problems with which organ?

9   The blood problem anaemia is sometimes cured by extra doses of which mineral?

10   Vitamin C is needed to prevent which disease?

Answers on page 164

1   Which of Jesus' disciples was the treasurer?

2   Who was the pacifist who led India's struggle for independence?

3   What name was given to members of the 'flower power' movement?

4   Which religion supports the caste system?

5   How did the suffragette Emily Davison die?

6   Whose teachings were used as a basis for the government of China for more than 2,000 years until 1912?

7   What do Buddhists call the attainment of perfect serenity?

8   In which book did Charles Darwin expound the idea of evolution?

9   Which book of the Bible describes the end of the world and the Last Judgement?

10   How many Noble Truths does Buddhism recognize?

Answers on page 164

1 The *Big Bang* refers to which event?

2 What name is given to the study of the beginning and development of the universe?

3 Which element is fuel for stars?

4 What name is given to a cloud of dust and gas floating in the universe?

5 A light year is a measure of what?

6 What name is given to a collection of millions of stars?

7 How many billion years old is the universe thought to be? a) 10–20 b) 20–30 c) 30–40

8 Where is the world's best telescope?

9 Which distinctive constellation is named after a hunter in Greek myth?

Answers on page 165

Film and TV   37

1   In which television series did Roger Moore star from
        1962 to 1970?

2   Who was the film director responsible for popularizing
        'spaghetti' westerns?

3   What was the Beatles' first film?

4   Who introduced the Betamax video cassette system?

5   Who starred in *Desperately Seeking Susan* and *Dick
        Tracy*?

6   Which former reform school boy starred in *Bullitt* and
        The Magnificent Seven?

7   Who won a 1993 Oscar for Best Actress in *The Piano*?

8   Who starred in *The Elephant Man* and *The Silence of
        the Lambs*?

9   In which country was Arnold Schwarzenegger born?

10   Who was the US producer responsible for *Tom and
        Jerry* films?

Answers on page 165

1   Which Baroque composer wrote *The Four Seasons*?

2   Beethoven, Dvorák and Vaughan Williams all wrote the same number of symphonies. How many?

3   On which instrument was Frédéric Chopin a virtuoso?

4   What is the name of the guitar-like Russian stringed instrument with a triangular body?

5   Which Viennese composer left his eighth symphony unfinished?

6   How many valves does a trumpet have?

7   Which opera did Bizet write just before his death in 1875?

8   Of what kind of dance did Johann Strauss become 'king' in the late 19th century?

9   Which female singing voice lies between soprano and contralto?

10   Which instrument does Nigel Kennedy play?

Answers on page 165

1   Where was William Shakespeare born?

2   What was the title of George Bernard Shaw's play about Joan of Arc?

3   Where in Germany was the Wagner theatre established in 1876?

4   Who is behind the character of Dame Edna Everage?

5   Who wrote and starred in *Hay Fever*, *Private Lives* and *Blithe Spirit*?

6   Who created the role of Archie Rice in *The Entertainer* and later had a London theatre named after him?

7   What is the subtitle of *Peter Pan*?

8   In which type of play is St George a major character?

9   Which traditional British form of entertainment combined harlequinade and burlesque?

10   What was the first free rock festival, held over three days in 1969?

Answers on page 165

What's in a Name?   40

1   Which name was shared by three of Henry VIII's wives?

2   Thomas Newcomen called his invention a 'fire engine', but what do we call it?

3   Who gave his name to the SI unit of electrical current?

4   What was the name of the ferry that capsized off Zeebrugge in 1987?

5   What name is given to the wild pansy?

6   What was the boxer Muhammad Ali's former name?

7   What is the modern name of the city once called Byzantium?

8   What is the American rocket launch site, once called Cape Kennedy, now called?

9   What was the assumed name of Jean François Gravelet, who crossed Niagara Falls on a tightrope?

10   What was the name of the group led by Bob Geldof from 1975 to 1986?

Answers on page 165

1   Which pollutant has damaged the ozone layer?

2   Which animal has been hunted almost to extinction because of its horn?

3   What name is given to the hard white material of elephant tusks?

4   Which gas, released by car exhausts, stops the blood haemoglobin from working properly?

5   Which chemical, commonly used to increase crop yield, sometimes contaminates drinking water?

6   *Rainbow Warrior* was sunk in 1989, during a protest against what?

7   Which of the Sun's harmful rays are filtered out by the ozone layer high up in the atmosphere?

8   Acid rain is caused by which polluting gas?

9   What device is added to a car's exhaust system to reduce pollution?

10   When you recycle a drinks can, which metal are you likely to be conserving?

Answers on page 166

On Wheels

1   Which company bought Alfa Romeo in 1985?

2   Which game of chance involves a rotating wheel with 36 segments?

3   Which saint's emblem is a wheel?

4   Which early civilization developed the potter's wheel?

5   At what speed do TGV trains travel a) 275 kph/ 170 mph b) 300 kph/185 mph c) 325 kph/200 mph?

6   What nationality was the racing driver Ayrton Senna?

7   Which maker in 1972 introduced safety tyres, which seal themselves after a puncture?

8   How many wheels had a hansom cab?

9   In which country is the purpose-built Monza motor-racing circuit?

10 Which famous car with front-wheel drive, transverse engine, and independent rubber suspension was introduced in 1959?

Answers on page 166

44

1   Which new city became the capital of Brazil in 1960?

2   Which islands were the subject of a war between Argentina and Britain in 1982?

3   In which country are the Angel Falls, the world's highest waterfall?

4   With which other island does Trinidad form a republic?

5   On which island is Cape Horn?

6   Which two South American countries have no sea-coast?

7   Which central American country did the USA invade in December 1989?

8   Which mountain stands at the entrance of the harbour at Rio de Janeiro?

9   Which country was ruled by the Duvalier family from 1957 to 1986?

10   Which sea lies at the Western end of the Panama Canal?

Answers on page 166

1 What is the name of the protective outer layer of trees?

2 What is the green pigment used by plants to trap sunlight?

3 Which acid is produced in large quantities by lemon trees?

4 Which gas do plants need for photosynthesis?

5 What name is given to the microscopic plants found in great numbers in rivers, lakes, and oceans?

6 What name is given to plants which do not drop their leaves in winter?

7 In the Bible, who tasted the forbidden fruit?

8 Which plant has flowers but no proper leaves?

9 Which European tree lives the longest?

10 Socrates was poisoned by a potion made from which plant?

Answers on page 166

1   Who played Inspector Clouseau in five *Pink Panther* films?

2   Which breed of dog was kept by monks to find lost travellers in the Alps?

3   Which detective figures in the novel *The Hound of the Baskervilles*?

4   In which continent do jaguars live?

5   Which English king was called Lion-Heart?

6   Which general of World War II was nicknamed 'the Desert Fox'?

7   In astrology, which two months are in the star sign Leo?

8   What is unusual about a Manx cat?

9   Which spotted dogs used to walk beside carriages to fend off highwaymen?

10   Which is the largest of the great cats?

Answers on page 166

Colours in Science 46

1   What colour is chlorophyll?

2   What colour is haemoglobin?

3   What colour is the surface of Mars?

4   What colour is the planet Neptune when viewed from Earth?

5   What colour is the longest wavelength of visible light?

6   The dye indigo can be obtained naturally from which kind of organism?

7   What colour is the mineral lazurite?

8   In which branch of science is the 'red shift' important?

9   When our Sun runs out of fuel it will briefly pour out which colour of light?

10   What name is given to the blue-green coating that forms as a natural patina on copper, bronze, and brass?

Answers on page 167

1   With which animals did Hannibal cross the Alps to Rome?

2   In which Indian city did 43 people die in the notorious Black Hole?

3   Which countries fought the Hundred Years' War?

4   Who became President of South Africa in 1994?

5   Besieging forces of which country left the wooden horse outside the gates of Troy?

6   Who was the first president of the USA?

7   Which Soviet foreign minister gave his name to a petrol bomb?

8   What important position did Dick Whittington hold from 1397 to 1398?

9   Where was Napoleon exiled in 1814–15?

10 Of which country did the playwright Václav Havel become president in 1989?

Answers on page 167

Myth and Magic

1   What was the name of King Arthur's seat?

2   What is the name of the winged horse in Greek mythology?

3   What magic object did Mozart write about in his opera?

4   Which tiny boy, immortalized by the Grimm brothers, later lent his name to a circus performer?

5   Who wrote the novel *Dracula*?

6   Who led the Argonauts in the search for the Golden Fleece?

7   Who was the Norse god of thunder?

8   Which Shakespearean title character committed murder after a prophecy by three witches?

9   What date is Hallowe'en?

10   In which city is the statue of Hans Christian Andersen's 'Little Mermaid'?

Answers on page 167

1   Who was the Lord Chancellor beheaded for refusing to recognize Henry VIII as head of the church?

2   In which city do people travel in water-buses called *vaporetti*?

3   What was the first name of the politician Gladstone, the composer Walton, and the reformer Wilberforce?

4   In which of the arts did Vaslav Nijinsky and Margot Fonteyn excel?

5   Which religious group migrated westward to the Great Salt Lake, Utah, in 1847?

6   Of which tribe was Goliath the champion?

7   How many people traditionally sing in a barbershop group?

8   Who led the Free French forces during World War II?

9   Which 18th-century dictionary compiler defined himself as a 'harmless drudge'?

10   In which country do the inhabitants speak Magyar?

Answers on page 167

Who, What, Where?

1   Who lives in the Vatican?

2   Who was the youngest person to be elected president of the USA?

3   What is Big Ben?

4   Who 'singed the King of Spain's beard' in 1587?

5   Where are the British Crown Jewels kept?

6   What was the name of Ho Chi Minh City before 1976?

7   Who ruled Rome in a triumvirate with Octavian and Lepidus?

8   What are shown every year at Crufts?

9   Where was St Paul converted by a vision?

10 What is the largest fast-food chain in the world?

Answers on page 167

MEDIUM

1   In which country is Transylvania, home of the vampire legends?

2   What is the eye defect strabismus?

3   Which king was dethroned by the Glorious Revolution?

4   Which country was founded by Muhammad Ali Jinnah?

5   Which is the busiest airport in France?

6   Which planet has two moons, Phobos and Deimos?

7   What name is given to the mistake of saying 'a scoop of Boy Trouts' instead of 'a troop of Boy Scouts'?

8   What surname links a Wimbledon champion, a blues guitarist, an author of horror stories, and a Canadian prime minister?

9   Which modern country did the Romans call Lusitania?

10   What colour are pistachio nuts?

Answers on page 168

1   Who was the first Englishman to put a dinosaur on show?

2   Who, referring to the principle of leverage, said, 'Give me the place to stand and I will move the Earth'?

3   What is 'Lamarckism'?

4   Which field of learning attracted the attention of the ancient Greek Galen?

5   Who said that scientific theories should be falsifiable?

6   Robert Oppenheimer is remembered for his work on which invention?

7   Which metaphysician developed the theory of calculus at the same time as did Newton?

8   Who developed the modern system of classifying plants and animals?

9   Who discovered X-rays?

10   Which radioactive element is named after the progenitor of the periodic table?

Answers on page 168

1   What was the name of the Black Prince?

2   What adjective connects 24 September 1869, 29 October 1929, and 19 October 1987?

3   What was the first name of the children's writer E Nesbit?

4   After which president was the Boulder Dam on the Colorado River renamed?

5   What name was given to armed Russians fighting behind the French lines in 1812?

6   Which poet's middle name was Bysshe?

7   Who was known as Hollywood's 'Love Goddess' in the 1940s?

8   What does the F in John F Kennedy stand for?

9   What nickname was given to Arthur Harris of the RAF in World War II?

10   Who was the female star of the 1993 film *In the Name of the Father*?

Answers on page 168

1   In which country did King Hassan II ascend the throne in 1961?

2   Which British general was killed at Khartoum in 1885?

3   On the border of which two countries is the Victoria Falls?

4   What is the name shared by the currency units of Algeria and Tunisia?

5   Which actor won an Academy Award for his performance in *The African Queen*?

6   From which European country did Angola achieve independence in 1975?

7   Who wrote the novel *Cry, the Beloved Country* about South Africa?

8   Which religion regards Emperor Haile Selassie of Ethiopia as the Messiah?

9   What is the name of the volcanic valley that runs from the Sinai peninsula to central Mozambique?

10   Which explorer was the first to reach the Cape of Good Hope?

Answers on page 168

1   Albert Einstein is best known for his work in which area of physics?

2   Caffeine stimulates which part of the body?

3   Which instrument is used by physicists to measure heat?

4   Which scale is used to give a measure of acidity and alkalinity?

5   Who won a Nobel prize for working out the chemical structure of insulin?

6   Which scientific unit gives a measure of electrical resistance?

7   Chromatic aberration is a common defect in which scientific instrument?

8   The behaviour of a stretched spring is described by which scientific law?

9   Proteins are broken down by the animal digestive system to form which molecules?

10   Hubble's constant is used in which area of science?

Answers on page 168

1   Which film gained Paul Newman an Oscar in 1986?

2   What colour are salmon's eggs?

3   How many does the blue ball score at snooker?

4   What are red giants?

5   Which celebrated actress and courtesan started her career as an orange seller?

6   Who wrote the jazz classic *Rhapsody in Blue*?

7   Whose World Series Cricket introduced coloured uniforms to the game?

8   What colourful new name did Francis Drake give his ship the *Pelican*?

9   What happened on Black Thursday, 29 October 1929?

10   Which world-famous tourist attraction is in Orange County, California?

Answers on page 168

1   In which country is the Great Hassan II Mosque, the
     largest in the world?

2   Who designed the Cenotaph in London?

3   In which country is the Owen Falls dam, which creates
     the world's largest reservoir capacity?

4   What did the Romans build at Ostia, Boulogne,
     Ravenna and Dover?

5   Which British seaside resort boasts a tower 500 ft
     high?

6   Why was the White House painted white?

7   What is the other name for Paris's modern art gallery,
     the Beaubourg?

8   Where is the Topkapi Palace?

9   Sydney Harbour Bridge is an example of which kind
     of bridge construction?

10   The great cathedral of Notre Dame at Chartres is a
     masterpiece of which style of architecture?

Answers on page 169

1   Who was King of England from 1016, of Denmark from 1018, and of Norway from 1028 until his death in 1035?

2   What did Louis XVIII of France call 'the politeness of kings'?

3   In which country did King Albert succeed his brother Baudouin in 1993?

4   Which king's lovers included Nell Gwyn, Lady Portsmouth and Lucy Walter?

5   Which English king was killed at the Battle of Bosworth?

6   Which country's king and queen financed Christopher Columbus' voyage of exploration in 1492?

7   Which earl was known as 'the Kingmaker' during the Wars of the Roses?

8   In which country did Queen Juliana abdicate in favour of her daughter Beatrix in 1980?

9   Which jazzman was known as the 'King of Swing'?

10   Who was Emperor of Germany throughout the First World War?

Answers on page 169

1   Which guitarist burned his guitar at the Monterey festival in 1967?

2   Which singer won an Oscar for acting in *From Here to Eternity*?

3   What instrument was played by jazzman Django Reinhardt?

4   Which country singer recorded an album at Folsom Prison in 1968?

5   Which rock star led Tin Machine?

6   Which jazz singer was nicknamed 'Lady Day'?

7   What is the title of Bruce Springsteen's 1975 album?

8   Which group has been fronted by guitarists Jerry Garcia and Bob Weir for three decades?

9   Which composer had long-standing partnerships with Lorenz Hart and Oscar Hammerstein II?

10   Who was the 'Forces' Sweetheart' of World War II?

Answers on page 169

1   In which year did Wall Street crash and Herbert
     Hoover become president of the USA?

2   Which year saw Nicolae Ceausescu overthrown in
     Romania and Jack Nicholson appearing in *Batman*?

3   Which year saw popes John Paul I and II elected and
     Princess Margaret divorced from Lord Snowdon?

4   In which year did England win soccer's World Cup
     and Bob Dylan release *Blonde on Blonde*?

5   In which year did the Allies mount the D-day invasion
     and Humphrey Bogart star in *To Have and Have Not*?

6   Which year saw the deaths of Pope John XXIII and
     John F Kennedy, and the flight of the first woman in
     space?

7   Which year saw an abortive coup against President
     Gorbachev, and Robert Maxwell found dead at sea?

8   In which year did Jesse Owens dominate the Berlin
     Olympics and Edward VIII abdicate?

9   In which year did Leonid Brezhnev die and Argentina
     and Britain fight a war over the Falkland Islands?

10   In which year did man first walk on the Moon and
     Georges Pompidou succeed Charles de Gaulle as
     president of France?

Answers on page 169

1   What nationality was Kurt Waldheim, secretary
    general of the United Nations from 1972 to 1981?

2   In which modern country are the ruins of Ephesus?

3   In which Italian city is the Rialto bridge?

4   Who was Nazi Germany's minister of propaganda?

5   What kind of sporting event is the Hawaii Ironman?

6   Which river flows through Washington DC?

7   Whose troops were known as *Ironsides*?

8   What colour is the fur of a mink?

9   Which is the first day of Lent?

10 Which cricketer set world records by scoring 61,237
    runs and 197 centuries?

Answers on page 169

1 What do baleen whales eat?

2 Which Hindu god is represented as elephant-headed?

3 What name is given to the study of animal behaviour?

4 In what state is a 'sessile' animal likely to be?

5 Which part of a beetle's body is a skeleton?

6 Where in an animal would you find a mandible?

7 How long is the gestation period of a duck-billed platypus?

8 What kind of an animal is a scorpion?

9 Which vertebrates have a skeleton of cartilage rather than bone?

10 What is the name of the food storage organ found in many birds?

Answers on page 169

1   Which 15th-century navigator discovered the sea route from Europe to India by the Cape of Good Hope?

2   Which major export of Bangladesh is used to make sacking?

3   Which country uses the ringgit as its currency?

4   Who was Emperor of Japan during World War II?

5   What is the capital of Hong Kong?

6   Who was supposed to have told the *Arabian Nights* tales?

7   Which country was suspended from the Arab League for ten years from 1979?

8   Which sea lies between China and Korea?

9   What is the holy city of Sikhism?

10   Which country is bounded by Saudi Arabia, Oman, the Gulf of Aden, and the Red Sea?

Answers on page 170

Human Body

1   What tube connects the kidney to the bladder?

2   Where in the human body do you find the alveoli?

3   A bone is joined to a muscle by which structure?

4   Where are red blood cells made?

5   What is the name for a red blood cell?

6   Which organ makes bile?

7   In which organ are faeces formed?

8   Which name is given to the heart chamber which receives blood?

9   What is the name of the protein which forms hair and nails?

10   What is the biggest bone in the body?

Answers on page 170

1   Which comic-strip hero was created by Jerome Siegel and Joseph Shuster in 1938?

2   Which playwright said in a 1960 revue 'Life is rather like a tin of sardines – we're all of us looking for the key'?

3   How were Peter Sellers, Harry Secombe and Spike Milligan collectively known?

4   Who was the original clown called 'Joey'?

5   What were the first names of Laurel and Hardy?

6   Which playwright wrote the black comedies *Loot* and *What the Butler Saw*?

7   Which studio produced such comedies as *Passport to Pimlico* and *Kind Hearts and Coronets*?

8   Who sang the comic songs 'Mr Wu' and 'Cleaning Windows'?

9   Which bespectacled silent-film comedian was famous for his cliff-hanging stunts?

10   Which school was created by the cartoonist Ronald Searle?

Answers on page 170

1   Which planet is the densest?

2   How many moons has Neptune?

3   Which is the second largest planet in the solar system?

4   Which planet possesses the Galilean satellites?

5   Which planet is covered with frozen methane?

6   Which planet has an atmosphere composed mainly of oxygen and nitrogen in a ratio of 1 to 4?

7   Which is the largest moon in the solar system?

8   Where would you find the Caloris Basin?

9   What is the name of the largest moon of Uranus?

10   Where would you find the Aphrodite Terra?

Answers on page 170

1   Who said 'Anyone who hates small dogs and children can't be all bad'?

2   In which children's story does a carpenter find 'a piece of wood that laughed and cried like a child'?

3   What did Henry Ford say was 'more or less bunk'?

4   Who said 'We are not amused'?

5   Which film star told reporters 'I want to be alone'?

6   Whose 1963 speech began 'I have a dream...'?

7   What did Alexander Pope think was 'a dangerous thing'?

8   Of which battle did Winston Churchill say 'Before... we never had a victory; after... we never had a defeat'?

9   Who telephoned Mr Watson and said 'Come here; I want you' on 7 March 1876?

10   Which children's writer said that breakfast cereal is 'made of all those little curly wooden shavings you find in pencil sharpeners'?

Answers on page 170

1   Fish use the lateral line system for sensing which kind of stimulus?

2   Which part of the ear helps you balance?

3   Which eye defect is caused by loss of elasticity of the lens?

4   What kind of eye-defect is myopia?

5   How many colour pigments are there in the human retina?

6   Which ear problem will a 'grommet' solve?

7   Which part of the eye is responsible for focusing the lens?

8   Which human sense organ may be sensitive to magnetic fields?

9   Which light-sensitive pigment in plants is involved in the regulation of flowering?

10   Which sense does the Venus Flytrap use in order to capture prey?

Answers on page 170

1   Which English poet became Poet Laureate in 1843?

2   What nationality is the novelist Gabriel García
     Márquez?

3   In Pirandello's play, how many characters are in
     search of an author?

4   Who wrote about a pig called the Empress of
     Blandings?

5   What was Oscar Wilde's only novel?

6   Who wrote the 1988 novel *Foucault's Pendulum*?

7   What nationality was the playwright Henrik Ibsen?

8   Whose servant was Sancho Panza?

9   Which medieval writer was brother-in-law to John of
     Gaunt?

10   Whose play became the basis for the musical *My Fair
     Lady*?

Answers on page 171

1   Who was voted the best footballer of the 1980s by the world's press?

2   Who was the youngest ever winner of a singles title at Wimbledon?

3   How many players are there in a baseball team?

4   Which British racing driver was never world champion, but was runner-up every year from 1955 to 1958?

5   Who had a record reign of more than eleven years as world heavyweight boxing champion?

6   Who won Wimbledon every year from 1976 to 1980?

7   Which Grand Prix team's world champions have included Emerson Fittipaldi, Niki Lauda, Alain Prost and Ayrton Senna?

8   What is the name of the method of training a horse to carry out a set routine of movements?

9   In which country is the Belmont Stakes horse race run?

10   In angling, what name is given to the revolving lures used to catch salmon and trout?

Answers on page 171

1   For what is the Booker Prize awarded?

2   Where does bossa nova dance music originate?

3   On which day of the week is Ascension Day?

4   To which fish family do pilchards and sardines belong?

5   Against which disease did Edward Jenner develop a vaccine around 1800?

6   Who was the last king of Lydia, famed for his wealth?

7   The Colossus of Rhodes was a statue of which Greek god?

8   Followers of which religion are expected to undertake a pilgramage known as *hajj*?

9   Which two countries are divided by the Kattegat sea passage?

10   What is the usual colour of an aircraft's black box?

Answers on page 171

1   What type of rock is granite?

2   What is the approximate circumference of the Earth?

3   What is the name given to the study of earthquakes?

4   Which mineral forms quartz?

5   What is the scientific scale for measuring the hardness of rocks?

6   Which gas in the atmosphere is responsible for increased global warming?

7   Which gas in the atmosphere can be turned into fertilizer by some microbes?

8   What does a barometer measure?

9   Someone who studies tectonics is probably an expert in which field?

10   What name is given to your angular distance on the Earth's surface relative to the equator?

Answers on page 171

1   Who was the Australian-born star of *The Charge of the Light Brigade* and *The Master of Ballantrae*?

2   Which long-serving Australian prime minister was in office from 1949 to 1966?

3   What is a bandicoot?

4   How many times did Rod Laver win the Wimbledon Men's Singles championship?

5   What was the former name of Tasmania?

6   What does *Aotearoa*, the Maori name for New Zealand, mean?

7   Which Nobel prizewinner from New Zealand discovered alpha, beta, and gamma rays?

8   What shape is the pitch for Australian Rules Football?

9   Which Australian opera singer made her debut in England in 1952?

10   What is the name of the arid coastal plain between Western and South Australia?

Answers on page 171

1   What was the first man-made fibre?

2   What is the essential ingredient of all wood?

3   What is limestone?

4   What is the main constituent of natural gas?

5   Which atom other than oxygen is found in a pure crystal of quartz?

6   What is the tip of the nose made of?

7   Tanning is used in the preparation of which material?

8   When King Midas touched any material it turned into which metal?

9   Which metallic element is combined with iron to make stainless steel?

10   Black-and-white photography relies on the chemical properties of which metal?

Answers on page 171

1   Of which island is Valletta the capital?

2   In which city does the Council of Europe sit?

3   Which two colours appear on the flag of Denmark?

4   In which Polish city was the Solidarity union formed in 1980?

5   In which Italian city would you find Leonardo's *Last Supper*?

6   In which autonomous region of Spain are the cities of Cádiz and Córdoba?

7   With which power did Bulgaria side in World War II?

8   Into which country were Bohemia and Moravia incorporated after World War I?

9   From which country did Iceland become independent in 1944?

10 In which capital city were the treaties signed that established the European Economic Community?

Answers on page 172

1   What kind of material is treated by 'tempering'?

2   The introduction of the pendulum greatly improved the accuracy of which kind of device?

3   Which device bends as the temperature changes?

4   The technique of dialysis is used in which type of medical technology?

5   A transgenic animal is liable to result from which type of technology?

6   What kind of effect is used by a solenoid switch?

7   Warp and weft are found in which kind of a machine?

8   What does the abbreviation AM mean?

9   What is a cyclotron?

10   In a front-engined motor car what is the name of the device which connects the drive shaft to the rear axle?

Answers on page 172

1   What was Jean Paul Marat doing when he was stabbed by Charlotte Corday?

2   What weapon was used to kill Leon Trotsky?

3   Who was killed by a bomb at an election rally near Madras?

4   In which country was Benigno Aquino assassinated at the airport on his return from exile in 1983?

5   Which country's royal family was killed at Ekaterinburg?

6   Who wrote *The Murders in the Rue Morgue*?

7   In the Bible, who was the father of the murderer Cain?

8   Who did Claus von Stauffenberg try to kill in 1944?

9   Which king did Guy Fawkes try to blow up?

10   What was the profession of John Wilkes Booth, the assassin of Abraham Lincoln?

Answers on page 172

1   Who devised the first general-purpose calculating machine?

2   What is the basic unit of memory?

3   Which type of memory is 'volatile'?

4   Who invented a test designed to reveal the moment when a machine becomes as intelligent as a human?

5   Which name is given to the computer processors which mimic the mechanics of the human brain?

6   Which medical condition sometimes occurs among the keyboarding community?

7   Text displayed graphically is described by which acronym?

8   Who invented the term 'cyberspace'?

9   An interpreter translates a program into which kind of language?

10   When was Windows 3 released?

Answers on page 172

1   Which British Prime Minister fell from office because of his repeal of the Corn Laws?

2   Who was the first president of France's Fifth Republic?

3   Which party did F W de Klerk represent as South African president?

4   In which year did Saddam Hussein's forces invade Kuwait?

5   Who was the USA's vice president in 1990?

6   What is the Irish house of representatives called?

7   Which government post did Winston Churchill hold from 1924 to 1929?

8   Which Elizabethan politician, philosopher and essayist was fined £40,000 for taking bribes?

9   Mario Soares became the first socialist president of which country in 1986?

10   Where did Stalin, Churchill, and Roosevelt complete plans for the United Nations in 1945?

Answers on page 172

1   Which English landscape artist painted *The Fighting Téméraire* and *Rain, Steam and Speed*?

2   How many paintings did Van Gogh sell in his lifetime?

3   Which great art gallery had a glass pyramid built in a courtyard in the 1980s?

4   What nationality was the painter Goya?

5   Which painting technique uses water-based paint on wet plaster?

6   Which 20th-century English poet was famous for his enthusiasm for Victorian and Edwardian architecture?

7   Which French artist moved to Tahiti to paint in 1891?

8   What is Joseph Niepce's place in the history of visual arts?

9   Who painted *Guernica*, a comment on atrocities in the Spanish Civil War?

10   In which Spanish city is Gaudí's still unfinished Church of the Holy Family?

Answers on page 172

1   Which Italian company founded by six brothers withdrew from motor racing in 1957?

2   What is the wind force of a hurricane?

3   What is a hurdy-gurdy?

4   How many squares are on a draughts (checkers) board?

5   What is the anatomical name for the large flat bone at the front of the chest?

6   What is the Richter scale used to measure?

7   Who led an unsuccessful rebellion against Queen Elizabeth 1 in 1601?

8   Which semi-divine Trojan prince abandoned Queen Dido of Carthage?

9   Where were the 1932 and 1984 Olympic Games?

10   To which bird family does the jay belong?

Answers on page 173

1 Which element ignites spontaneously in normal air?

2 Which element was discovered to have a link with Alzheimer's disease?

3 Which radioactive element is the densest known gas?

4 Which element is the second most abundant in the universe?

5 Which poisonous yellow gas is commonly used in refrigerants?

6 Bauxite is the ore of which element?

7 Which element is mixed with copper to make bronze?

8 Which element is used in vulcanizing rubber?

9 Which element, used to make brass in the Bronze Age, was not recognized as a separate metal until 1746?

10 Which element is used by water companies and toothpaste manufacturers to protect teeth?

Answers on page 173

1   In which river would you find the Thousand Islands?

2   Which city was the first capital of the USA?

3   Which of the United States is bordered by California and New Mexico?

4   Which British general captured Québec in 1759, but died in the attempt?

5   Who was prime minister of Canada from 1968 to 1979 and from 1980 to 1984?

6   Who made history at Kitty Hawk, North Carolina, in 1903?

7   What did Captain Cook call Hawaii?

8   What was Abraham Lincoln doing when he was shot?

9   In which state is Yosemite National Park?

10   Which is the largest Canadian province in area?

Answers on page 173

1   Which medicine is extracted from the bark of the cinchona tree?

2   An embolism is a blockage. But where?

3   Multiple sclerosis is a disease of which system?

4   Beta-blockers affect which organ of the body?

5   Osteoporosis affects which part of the body?

6   What vitamin is used to cure the disease beriberi?

7   Diabetes is caused by a malfunction of cells in which organ of the body?

8   Barium sulphate is taken into the body by which method?

9   Interferon defends the body from which kind of microbe attack?

10   IVF is a form of therapy for which medical problem?

Answers on page 173

1   Which ancient Greek philosopher thought that knowledge emerges through dialogue and systematic questioning?

2   Which Christian festival celebrates the coming of the Magi?

3   What is the highest title in the Shi'ite sect of Islam?

4   Which astronomer said 'Finally we shall place the Sun himself at the centre of the Universe'?

5   How many lines make up each of the 64 patterns in the *I Ching*?

6   Which country do Rastafarians regard as the promised land?

7   What is the stage before full sainthood?

8   In which century did Roman Catholics declare the Pope infallible?

9   Which emperor disavowed his divinity in 1946?

10 What, in Hinduism, is the sum of a person's actions, which affects his or her fate in their next life?

Answers on page 174

1   Which force is nothing more than the bending of space and time?

2   Scientists study the red shift to investigate which aspect of cosmology?

3   Which star is as bright as 23 Suns, and is orbited by the Pup?

4   What is the defining feature of a neutron star?

5   What name was given to the invisible material once thought to occupy all space?

6   What name is given to the explosive death of a star?

7   What is the most distant object visible to the naked eye?

8   What is Betelgeuse?

9   Which is the second lightest element in the universe?

10 Which scientist first determined how stars make elements?

Answers on page 174

1   Which world-famous cartoon cat was created in 1920 by Pat Sullivan?

2   By what name is Bernard Schwartz better known?

3   Which film did Barbra Streisand direct in 1983?

4   To whom is Mae West popularly (but wrongly) supposed to have said 'Come up and see me some time' in *She Done Him Wrong*?

5   Which 1987 film earned an Academy Award for Bernardo Bertolucci?

6   What nationality was Lucille Ball's husband Desi Arnaz?

7   Which was Sean Connery's first James Bond film?

8   Why was Ingrid Bergman ostracized by Hollywood for many years?

9   Who wrote the screenplay for the film *A Private Function*?

10   Which pop star appeared in Nicholas Roeg's film *The Man Who Fell to Earth*?

Answers on page 174

1   Which scientist won the Nobel Prize for Chemistry *and* the Nobel Peace Prize?

2   Whose research on X-ray diffraction of DNA crystals helped Crick and Watson during the race to discover the structure of DNA?

3   Who persuaded Einstein to write to President F D Roosevelt of the USA, warning him of the power of atomic fission?

4   Which scientist discovered the neutron?

5   Who was the first scientist to win Nobel Prizes for Physics *and* Chemistry?

6   Einstein left Germany to work at which American university?

7   Heisenberg is most associated with which branch of physics?

8   Stephen Jay Gould developed which evolutionary theory?

9   What did Heike Kamerlingh-Onnes discover?

10   Which scientist wrote the science-fiction novel *The Black Cloud*?

Answers on page 174

1   Who became conductor of the Birmingham Symphony Orchestra at the age of 25 in 1980?

2   Which instrument did Bartolommeo Cristofori invent in 1704?

3   What nationality was the composer Jean Sibelius?

4   Which Russian composer wrote *Peter and the Wolf*?

5   Which conductor said 'The English may not like music, but they absolutely love the noise it makes'?

6   Who wrote Italian and Scottish symphonies?

7   Who turned his score for the film *Scott of the Antarctic* into his *Sinfonia Antarctica*?

8   Which play by the French dramatist de Beaumarchais did Rossini turn into an opera?

9   Who wrote the *Moonlight* and *Appassionata* among his 32 piano sonatas?

10 Who wrote *Prélude à l'Après-midi d'un Faune*?

Answers on page 174

1   Discovery of the remains of which London theatre, where many of Shakespeare's plays were performed, caused controversy in 1989?

2   Whose shows included *Gay's the Word* and *Glamorous Night*?

3   In which Gilbert and Sullivan operetta was Oscar Wilde's dandyism parodied?

4   Where can a theatre named after Gracie Fields be found?

5   Who wrote the lyrics for *West Side Story*?

6   Which famous actor was a pupil of Dr Johnson?

7   Which show contains the song 'Ol' Man River'?

8   Which playwright's first successful novel, *The Good Companions,* was about a travelling theatre company?

9   What is the nickname of Broadway, New York?

10 Which contemporary playwright acted in the films *The Right Stuff* and *Steel Magnolias*?

Answers on page 174

1   Which Rolls-Royce car was produced between 1906 and 1925?

2   Which famous steam locomotive inaugurated the first passenger railway line?

3   In which field was Sir Mortimer Wheeler famous?

4   Which two activities beside cycling are involved in the triathlon?

5   Who produced the world's first petrol-driven motor vehicle?

6   Where did William Morris begin manufacturing cars in 1910?

7   What does TT mean in the Isle of Man's TT motor cycle races?

8   Which was France's first mass-producer of cars?

9   What was the former name of the Tour of Britain cycle race?

10   By what name is Ferdinand Porsche's 'people's car' better known?

Answers on page 175

1   Which Canadian city gave its name to the 1987 world agreement on protection of the ozone layer?

2   The damaged Chernobyl nuclear power station is situated in which country?

3   What name is given to the huge growths of algae sometimes seen in polluted lakes and rivers?

4   Which town in northern India is unfortunately best known for a disastrous chemical leak which killed 2,600 people?

5   What was the name of the dioxin-containing defoliant used during the Vietnam War by the USA army?

6   Five-legged creatures have damaged which 2,000-km-long wonder of the world?

7   In which area of the world do tropical rainforests occur?

8   Who compared the world to a living organism?

9   CITES is an international agreement on which environmental problem?

10   The dodo was a native bird of which island?

Answers on page 175

1 Which South American leader was known as 'the Liberator'?

2 What is the meaning of Sendero Luminoso, the name of the Peruvian guerrilla group?

3 Of which European country was Surinam once a colony?

4 Which country shares the island of Hispaniola with Haiti?

5 Which two countries have shores on Lake Titicaca?

6 In which country has the city of Medellín become a centre for the drugs trade?

7 What was Evita Duarte's profession before she married Juan Perón?

8 Where in Cuba did the USA sponsor an abortive invasion in 1961?

9 In which country was Che Guevara born?

10 What is the capital of Guatemala?

Answers on page 175

1 Which tissue carries sugary sap around the plant?

2 Mosses are classified as belonging to which part of the plant kingdom?

3 Which cells form the middle layer of plant leaves?

4 Photosynthesis is carried out in which part of the cell?

5 Which part of a plant may be sinuate?

6 The maidenhair tree is the sole survivor of which class of plant?

7 Which sub-division of plants is named after their practice of forming 'naked seeds'?

8 Which part of the common valerian is used to make a sedative?

9 What is the name of the structures which allow leaves to breathe?

10 What is the name of the structures which allow stems to breathe?

Answers on page 175

1   How many canine teeth does a human have?

2   What is another name for a mountain lion?

3   Who was the female star of the 1965 film *Cat Ballou*?

4   What is the smallest breed of dog?

5   Who made a voyage of discovery to the Galápagos Islands aboard HMS *Beagle*?

6   Which variety of dog originating in America cannot be imported, bred, or sold in Britain under laws passed in 1989 and 1991?

7   Who wrote the music for *Cats*?

8   What is a fox's den called?

9   A famous George Stubbs painting shows which animal attacking a horse?

10   How many heads did Cerberus, the dog who guarded Hades, have?

Answers on page 175

1   What was shown by the Michelson-Morley experiment?

2   The astronomer Edwin Hubble used his measurements of the Doppler effect to study which aspect of the universe?

3   Where is the world's most powerful particle accelerator?

4   Which name was given to the World War II American project that successfully developed the atomic bomb?

5   What was the age of the first human to receive gene therapy?

6   Which Greek philosopher threw himself into the crater of Mt Etna as part of an experiment to observe the lifting effects of hot air?

7   Which ancient Greek made a discovery and jumped from the bath?

8   Who introduced dissection to the medical colleges of Europe?

9   Which English priest first demonstrated the upward movement of water through plant vascular tissue?

10 Who first demonstrated that white light is a mixture of colours?

Answers on page 175

1   In which year did Dublin's Easter Rising take place?

2   Which family ruled Florence for three centuries from 1434?

3   Which British monarch married Anne of Denmark?

4   What title did Charlemagne, already king of the Franks, acquire in 800?

5   What was the first permanent English settlement in the New World, now in ruins?

6   Who proclaimed the People's Republic of China in 1949?

7   Which country first tried unsuccessfully to build the Panama Canal?

8   In which industrial process was the inventor Joseph Arkwright responsible for an important breakthrough in 1768?

9   Who was the first president of independent Kenya?

10   Which country sold land including the present-day states of Louisiana, Arkansas, and Oklahoma to the USA in 1803?

Answers on page 176

1   What are magic bullets?

2   Whom did Orpheus try to rescue from the realm of the dead?

3   What would be your zodiac sign if you were born on New Year's Day?

4   What creature's head did Anubis, the Egyptian god of the dead, have?

5   What was the name of a one-eyed Sicilian giant in Greek mythology?

6   Which sign of the zodiac is represented by the scales of justice?

7   To which British monarch was *The Faerie Queene* dedicated?

8   In which river does the Lorelei lure sailors onto a rock?

9   In Greek mythology, who was fated to make true prophecies that were never believed?

10   Which poem tells of a sailor cursed for shooting an albatross?

Answers on page 176

1   Which warship's wreck was raised in 1982, 437 years after it had sunk?

2   In which country are the Sutherland Falls?

3   Which capital city is close to Waterloo?

4   What percentage of the human body is made up of water?

5   Who wrote *Watership Down*?

6   In which country is Lake Guatavita, the source of the legend of 'El Dorado'?

7   How many players are in the water at one time in a water polo match?

8   The male of which species of whale, found only in the Arctic Ocean, possesses a spiral tusk up to 9 ft long?

9   For what product is the Irish town of Waterford famous?

10   Which is the second largest of the Great Lakes?

Answers on page 176

1   Who was Henry VIII's first wife?

2   Who succeeded Hitler in 1945?

3   Whose birthday is celebrated by a public holiday on the third Monday in January in the USA?

4   Who was the American politician who made wild claims of communist infiltration in the 1950s?

5   Which surname is shared by two US presidents and a world heavyweight boxing champion?

6   Which builder of steam engines formed a successful partnership with Matthew Boulton?

7   Of which country was de Valera the prime minister, and later the president?

8   What nationality was the spy Mata Hari?

9   What did Herbert Austin begin manufacturing at Northfield, Birmingham in 1905?

10 How did the dancer Isadora Duncan die?

Answers on page 176

HARD

1   Of which kind of computer program was VisiCalc the first?

2   Which former astronaut was elected senator for Ohio in 1974?

3   Which religion has five duties called the 'five pillars'?

4   Which bodily organ's functions can be taken by an artificial device called a haemodializer?

5   Which Brazilian dance became fashionable in Europe in 1989?

6   What is a fennec?

7   Whose last major painting was *A Bar at the Folies-Bergère*?

8   In which English county is Piltdown, site of a famous archaeological hoax?

9   In semaphore, what letter is indicated by one flag held straight up and one flag held straight down?

10   Which African country has a land border with only one other country, Senegal?

Answers on page 177

1   What type of scientist might come across 'the uncertainty principle'?

2   Uniformitarianism is a theory from which field of science?

3   The physician William Harvey studied at which Italian university?

4   Who developed a theory of continental drift?

5   The Livermore Laboratory is part of which university?

6   Which Marxist psychoanalyst wrote *The Function of the Orgasm*?

7   Who named oxygen?

8   Who first described the cell nucleus?

9   The physicist Francis Aston is credited with developing which scientific instrument?

10   Who discovered that the universe is expanding?

Answers on page 177

1　What is blue john?

2　What stage name did the French actress and dancer Jeanne Bourgeois take?

3　What does the K in Jerome K Jerome stand for?

4　What was the name of the jet-powered car that took Richard Noble to the land-speed record in 1983?

5　Which planet has a moon named after a Shakespearean queen of the fairies?

6　Which Italian author wrote *The Name of the Rose*?

7　What was the name of the spacecraft that carried Yuri Gagarin on the first manned flight?

8　What is the common name of Risso's dolphin?

9　What name is given to a baseball player who bats both left- and right-handed?

10　Which film star started his career in 1927 under the name Duke Morrison?

Answers on page 177

1   Which country includes the Yoruba, Ibo, and Hausa-
     Fulani peoples?

2   After which American president is the capital of
     Liberia named?

3   In which township were 69 demonstrators killed by
     South African police in March 1960?

4   Which country's capital city is Niamey?

5   Which country ruled Sudan from 1820 to 1881?

6   In and around which desert do the Bushmen live?

7   What appears in the middle of the Rwandan flag?

8   In which present-day country was the ancient city of
     Carthage?

9   Which is Africa's largest city?

10   Which South African politician won the Nobel Peace
     Prize in 1960?

Answers on page 177

1   What name is given to the study of very low
     temperatures?

2   Who founded the science of electromagnetism?

3   Which protein forms the main constituent of an
     insect's exoskeleton?

4   Corundum is a mineral oxide of which metal?

5   Where would you find a Golgi body?

6   Ornithophily is what?

7   Mars has how many moons?

8   What name is given to the development of the
     individual?

9   Potassium belongs to which group of elements?

10   What is *Solanum tuberosum*?

Answers on page 177

1   Who wrote *The Scarlet Letter*?

2   What was the birthplace of naturalist Gilbert White, immortalized in his best-known book?

3   *Tom Brown's Schooldays* provided a fictionalized portrait of the headmaster of which great English public school?

4   What colour are halides, the light-sensitive compounds used to coat photographic film?

5   What kind of creature is a green darner?

6   What colour shirts were worn by the followers of Garibaldi?

7   Which king of England was nicknamed 'the Red'?

8   Which English composer wrote *A Colour Symphony* in 1922?

9   What is the red dye cochineal obtained from?

10 Who is the father of Lady Rose Windsor, born in 1980?

Answers on page 177

1   Who almost beat Darwin to the theory of natural selection?

2   Which American physicist directed the development of the atomic bomb and was later accused of being a security risk?

3   Controversial scientific results announced in 1989, yet never achieved, suggested a new source of limitless, cheap energy. But what were the scientists investigating?

4   Who introduced the term 'eugenics'?

5   Which discredited technique used the shape of the skull as a method of measuring intelligence?

6   Which English educational psychologist was accused of fabricating his results?

7   Who accused Marxism of being 'unscientific'?

8   Whose theory of continental drift languished unloved?

9   Which scientist won the Nobel Peace Prize for his campaigning against the atomic bomb?

10   Which Stalin-sponsored geneticist prevented the growth of Mendel's ideas in the USSR?

Answers on page 178

1   Where did King Zog reign from 1928 to 1939?

2   On which island did Queen Victoria die?

3   'Good King Wenceslas' was actually a Duke, but of which country?

4   Which disease was known as the king's evil?

5   French kings nicknamed the Bald, the Simple, the Fair, and the Mad shared which name?

6   Which queen of England was prevented from entering Westminster Abbey for her husband's coronation?

7   Which royal family ruled Austria from 1278 until 1918?

8   Which of Alexander the Great's generals became king of Egypt?

9   In which country did a communist-led coalition force King Michael to abdicate in 1947?

10   Which English kingdom was ruled by Offa from 757 to 796?

Answers on page 178

1   What was Bing Crosby's real first name?

2   Who released the album *Natty Dread* in 1975?

3   Which Memphis label recorded both Elvis Presley and Johnny Cash?

4   Which rock group's original pianist Ian Stewart died in 1985?

5   Who wrote the atmospheric scores for such films as *A Fistful of Dollars* and *The Good, the Bad and the Ugly*?

6   Which pop group once consisted of Sarah Dallin, Keren Woodward and Jackie O'Sullivan?

7   Which 1965 Beatles song was covered by 1,186 performers in ten years?

8   In which American state were both Buddy Holly and Janis Joplin born?

9   Who made the jazz albums *Birth of the Cool* and *Sketches of Spain*?

10 What stage name was taken by the rapper Stanley Kirk Burrell?

Answers on page 178

1   In which year did Sputnik I become the first artificial satellite, and Harold Macmillan become British prime minister?

2   Which year saw Scott of the Antarctic's last expedition and the sinking of the *Titanic*?

3   In which year was the wreck of the *Titanic* found and the Greenpeace ship *Rainbow Warrior* sunk?

4   In which year did Mao Zedong found the People's Republic and China and the USSR lift the Berlin blockade?

5   In which year did Richard Nixon resign as US president and Tom Stoppard's *Travesties* appear?

6   In which year did Fidel Castro overthrow the Batista regime in Cuba and Buddy Holly die in a plane crash?

7   Which year saw Margaret Thatcher elected leader of the Conservative party and Arthur Ashe win Wimbledon?

8   In which year was Prohibition lifted and Hitler appointed chancellor of Germany?

9   In which year did the Rolling Stones release 'Satisfaction' and Aleksei Leonov make the first space walk?

10   In which year did Jimmy Carter lose a presidential election and Bjorn Borg win his fifth and last Wimbledon title?

Answers on page 178

1   Which virus was identified, separately, by Robert Gallo and Luc Montagnier?

2   In Tibet, what are hard slabs of tea used as before being brewed?

3   Which real-life Elizabethan hero is satirized in Shakespeare's *Love's Labours Lost*?

4   What is the real first name of the tycoon Tiny Rowland?

5   In Japan, what is a koto?

6   Who won an Oscar for his performance in *Kiss of the Spider Woman* in 1985?

7   In which sport would you compete for Doggett's Coat and Badge?

8   Which island is known to the Greeks as Kérkira?

9   Who wrote the verse dramas *The Lady's Not for Burning* and *A Sleep of Prisoners*?

10 Who built the first jet aircraft?

Answers on page 178

1   What is a tragopan?

2   What kind of specialist would study storm petrels?

3   Which kind of organisms are likely to show a 'taxis'?

4   Where in a vertebrate would you find the protein myoglobin?

5   What is the name of the evolutionary theory suggesting that evolution has an uneven pace?

6   What is the name of the so-called 'first bird'?

7   What is a hackney?

8   In animal classification, how are the phyla subdivided?

9   How many species of domestic dog are found today?

10   What kind of animal is a barnacle?

Answers on page 178

1   What distinguished the Japanese tanker *Shin-Aitoku-Maru*, launched in 1980?

2   Which country is made up of 13,677 islands?

3   A 25-km causeway, the longest in the world, links Saudi Arabia with which other country?

4   What does the Japanese word 'kamikaze' mean?

5   Isfahan is a major city in which country?

6   Beside which river are the Indian cities of Delhi and Agra?

7   What is the Japanese product kakiemon?

8   The dong is which country's currency unit?

9   What is the dominant classical language of the Indian subcontinent?

10   Of which country is Vientiane the capital?

Answers on page 179

1   When the egg is released from the ovary, what is left behind?

2   Where is the sinoatrial node?

3   Which hormone helps control ovulation?

4   Where would you find the carotid arteries?

5   Which organ destroys old red blood cells?

6   The pituitary controls many hormones. But what controls the pituitary?

7   Where would you find the islets of Langerhans?

8   How many distinct bones are there in a human skeleton? a) 163 b) 187 c) 206?

9   Which gland secretes the corticosteroids?

10   Which part of the body produces the excretory product urea?

Answers on page 179

1   Which comedian of silent films was ruined in 1921 by
       a sex scandal?

2   Under what stage name did Maxwell George Lister do
       his funny walk?

3   Which magazine carried the ghoulish cartoons of
       Charles Addams, featuring the Addams family?

4   Who in the 1920s wrote such Aldwych farces as *A
       Cuckoo in the Nest* and *Rookery Nook*?

5   Which humorist wrote 'The Secret Life of Walter
       Mitty'?

6   Which master of slapstick created the Keystone Cops?

7   Which long-running British humorous magazine was
       founded in 1841?

8   Which cartoon strip is drawn by Garry Trudeau?

9   Which of the Marx Brothers was really named Arthur?

10   Which cartoon character is actually a *geococcyx
       californianus*?

Answers on page 179

1   Saturn's ring has how many sections?

2   Which planet is composed of an inner core, a mantle, and an outer crust?

3   When was the first *Pioneer* space probe?

4   Which was the first crewed *Apollo* spacecraft to orbit the Earth?

5   Proteus and Nereid are moons of which planet?

6   Europa is a moon of which planet?

7   Which gas gives Neptune its blue colour?

8   Who discovered Uranus?

9   Jupiter is largely composed of hydrogen and which other gas?

10   Which was the last *Apollo* mission?

Answers on page 179

1   Which of Scott Fitzgerald's novels was unfinished at the time of his death?

2   Complete the Graham Greene novel title: *The Heart of* ...

3   Which Roman poet wrote *Metamorphoses*?

4   Complete the Beatrix Potter book title: *The Tailor of* ...

5   What relation to each other were Rabelais' giants Gargantua and Pantagruel?

6   Which English poet planned a Communist colony in America with Robert Southey?

7   Whose novels include *The Aunt's Story* and *The Tree of Man*?

8   Which American writer was court-martialled in 1830 for neglect of duty?

9   Who wrote *Boris Godunov*?

10   Complete the title of this Ionesco play: *The Bald* ...

Answers on page 179

1   How long, exactly, is a marathon?

2   In which city is the Wanderers' cricket ground?

3   What are the two standard lifts in international weightlifting competitions?

4   Of what would you find types called Finn, Tornado and Windglider?

5   In which country did chess originate?

6   Which sport was started by James Plympton in Newport, Rhode Island, in 1866?

7   Which England cricketer scored a record 456 runs in a test match in 1990?

8   Why was Muhammad Ali stripped of his world heavyweight boxing title in 1967?

9   Which sport was originally called Mintonette?

10   Which was the earliest of the English classic horse races?

Answers on page 179

1   How many flavours has the quark?

2   Each flavour of quark comes in how many colours?

3   Which is the antiparticle of the electron?

4   Which particle in the nucleus carries no charge?

5   Which particle has a charge of minus one?

6   Which type of particle is not affected by the strong nuclear force?

7   Which particle has a mass too small to measure?

8   Which is the fundamental particle making up all hadrons?

9   Who first recognized the nuclear nature of the atom?

10 Which particle in the atomic nucleus has a charge of plus one?

Answers on page 180

1   Where might you find an aurora?

2   What name is given to the rocks swallowed by dinosaurs to assist their digestion?

3   Which of the Earth's atmospheric layers reflects radio waves?

4   What atom, released by atmospheric CFCs, causes damage to the ozone layer?

5   What name is given to the rock formations used as a source of water?

6   Which radioactive substance sometimes occurs naturally in spring water?

7   Where are you likely to come across a laccolith?

8   What kind of a person might study a podzol?

9   What type of rock is formed by the rapid cooling of molten lava?

10   Which quarry in the Italian region of Tuscany is renowned for the quality of its marble?

Answers on page 180

1   With which of the arts was Frederick Ashton involved?

2   With which philosophy is the French novelist Albert Camus associated?

3   In which country was Buddha born?

4   Who is the patron saint of painters?

5   Who was the king of the fairies in folklore?

6   The two main systems of which martial art are *tomiki* and *uyeshiba*?

7   Who was the first fashion designer to sell ready-to-wear collections to department stores?

8   What does Mohs' Scale measure?

9   In which country is the world's oldest parliament?

10 How is the writer Jean-Baptiste Poquelin better known?

Answers on page 180

1   Who designed the Sydney Opera House?

2   Which two Australian explorers made the first south to north crossing of the country?

3   Which Australian-born author wrote *The Female Eunuch*?

4   Which river forms the boundary between New South Wales and Victoria, flowing into the sea at Encounter Bay?

5   Who, true to form, provoked a mutiny as governor of New South Wales in 1808?

6   Where in Australia was the world water speed record set in 1964?

7   Where was the America's Cup hosted in 1987?

8   Which novel won the Booker Prize for Australian writer Thomas Keneally in 1982?

9   Which great aviator is thought to have died of thirst on Nikumaroro Island, southeast of Kiribati's main island group, after disappearing on a Pacific flight in 1937?

10   Which two Australian states never received transported convicts?

Answers on page 180

1   American designer Louis Comfort Tiffany is famous for his work in which material?

2   What kind of a material is 'Quorn'?

3   Rusting produces which material?

4   Tungsten gets its name from the words 'heavy stone'. But in which language?

5   Camphor is what type of chemical?

6   Which material is produced by the Haber process?

7   What is the name of the material found inside living cells but outside the nucleus?

8   The first florin, minted in 1252, was composed of which material?

9   What kind of rock is the Rosetta stone?

10 What was the first synthetic plastic?

Answers on page 180

1   Which poet died while helping the Greeks fight for their independence?

2   Which country was defeated by the USSR in the 'Winter War' of 1939?

3   Which crusade was led by Philip II Augustus of France and Richard I of England?

4   In Norway, what are Hardanger and Sogne?

5   On which river does Prague stand?

6   What emblem appears on the flag of Albania?

7   In which country did Grand Duke Jean become head of state in 1964?

8   What nationality was the 16th-century poet and soldier Camoëns?

9   What was the name of the ship of the French oceanographer Jacques Cousteau?

10   On which of the Greek islands did Bacchus find Ariadne, according to legend?

Answers on page 181

1   The bobbing device invented by Stephen Salter to harness wave power was named after which bird?

2   What was the occupation of Robert Stirling, inventor of the Stirling Engine?

3   Where in aeroplanes are the ailerons positioned?

4   When was the first transatlantic telephone cable laid?

5   Spinnerets are used in the manufacture of which type of material?

6   What name is given to the technique of moulding metal?

7   In the baking industry fermentation is used to produce which gas?

8   Which technology is commonly used for checking the growth of the fetus?

9   The external-combustion engine is best seen in which type of engine?

10 Which part of the motor-car engine provides the high-tension current necessary for sparking?

Answers on page 181

1   Who was poisoned, then shot, then dumped in the
      river Neva in 1916?

2   Who was Irish head of state for 10 days until he was
      killed in an ambush?

3   Which murderer was the first to be caught by the use
      of radio?

4   Which British prime minister was shot dead in the
      lobby of the House of Commons?

5   Which US president had been in office only four
      months when he was assassinated?

6   Who was the black nationalist leader assassinated by
      Black Muslims in Harlem in 1965?

7   Which pre-Norman English king was murdered at
      Corfe Castle?

8   Where in Rome was Julius Caesar assassinated?

9   Which American hero's infant son was kidnapped and
      murdered in 1932?

10   On which religious festival did Catherine de Medici
      have thousands of Huguenots killed in Paris in 1572?

Answers on page 181

1   Whose book *Sexual Politics* was a landmark in feminist thinking?

2   Who ranks immediately above an earl in the British peerage?

3   Of which party is Benazir Bhutto the leader?

4   Which policy helped Pierre Trudeau to a landslide victory in the Canadian presidential election of 1980?

5   Which publication was the vehicle for John Wilkes's attacks on the Tories for which he was imprisoned?

6   Who was dismissed from office as Australian Prime Minister in 1975 after refusing to call a general election?

7   Whose book *Inside No 10* described Harold Wilson's Downing Street years?

8   Which American president extended the New Deal into the Fair Deal?

9   In which year did Mikhail Gorbachev resign as Soviet president?

10   Whom did Col Khaddhafi overthrow to become Libyan leader in 1969?

Answers on page 181

1   Where in the cell are the genes stored?

2   What are gene shears used for cutting?

3   What protein-manufacturers receive messenger RNA?

4   Which name is given to the position on a chromosome where a gene resides?

5   What is the scientific name for a triplet of bases on the DNA molecule?

6   In DNA what is the pairing base for cytosine?

7   The recessive gene for haemophilia is carried on which chromosome?

8   The DNA backbone comprises sugar and which other molecule?

9   Which is the commonest genetically inherited medical disorder?

10   In DNA what is the pairing base for adenine?

Answers on page 181

1   Which French impressionist painter was famous for his studies of ballet, horse racing, and young women working?

2   Which English architect's masterpiece is the Banqueting House in Whitehall, London?

3   Which American National Park was the subject of many of Ansel Adams' greatest photographs?

4   Whose paintings *Raising of the Cross* and *Descent from the Cross* are in Antwerp Cathedral?

5   Which painter was given his nickname because his father was a dyer?

6   Which artist, more famous as a sculptor, made drawings of people in London's air-raid shelters during World War II?

7   What is the acronym for using computers to create and edit design drawings?

8   Which European capital city has the Atomium, an iron model of an atom enlarged many billions of times?

9   Which children's stories are illustrated by E H Shepard?

10 Who is the Bulgarian-born sculptor who specializes in wrapping very large objects, like buildings and bridges?

Answers on page 181

1   Which explorer's last words were 'I am just going outside, and may be some time'?

2   What did Le Corbusier call 'a machine for living in'?

3   What did James Bryce describe in 1912 as 'the greatest liberty that Man has ever taken with Nature'?

4   What did Elbert Hubbard call 'just one damned thing after another'?

5   Who said 'If one tells the truth, one is sure, sooner or later, to be found out'?

6   What did Marshall McLuhan call 'the greatest art form of the twentieth century'?

7   Complete Henry Thoreau's quote: 'The mass of men lead lives of quiet...'

8   Who said 'No man is good enough to govern another without that other's consent'?

9   Which document declares 'To no man will we sell, or deny, or delay, right or justice'?

10 What philosphy's first principle, according to one of its chief exponents, is 'Man is nothing else but what he makes of himself'?

Answers on page 182

1 Which founder member of the Royal Academy is famous for portraits of Mrs Siddons, David Garrick, and Dr Johnson?

2 Who is the Greek goddess of war?

3 In which city was Mussolini hanged with his mistress in a public square in 1945?

4 Which famous screen actor was born Issur Danielovitch?

5 Which order of classical column has leaves in the capital?

6 What sort of religious building derives its name from the Latin word for 'seat'?

7 Who created the famous gardens at Sissinghurst?

8 What is a frogmouth?

9 Where is the Vincent van Gogh Museum?

10 Who built the first steam engine to run on rails?

Answers on page 182

1   What type of element is arsenic?

2   Which element is important for the proper functioning of the thyroid gland?

3   Which element is an essential constituent of the green plant pigment chlorophyll?

4   Which element, apart from hydrogen, is found in an amine group?

5   Which element is named after the Greek word for 'odour'?

6   What is the third most abundant metal in the world?

7   Which is the most electropositive of all the elements?

8   Fluorite is a mineral containing fluorine and which other element?

9   What is the atomic number of magnesium?

10   Pitchblende is an important source of which element?

Answers on page 182

1   What is the mainland part of Newfoundland called?

2   What new name was given to Bedloe's Island in 1956?

3   What was the surname of the grandfather and grandson who became presidents of the USA?

4   Where in Texas is the Alamo?

5   Who was the last Aztec king, killed in 1520 by the Spanish?

6   Which of the United States is nicknamed the First State?

7   What was the name of the provisional government of the USA during the American Revolution?

8   Which is the highest of the Rocky Mountains?

9   Who wrote the song 'God Bless America' in 1939?

10   In which city did Berry Gordy set up his Motown record company in 1959?

Answers on page 182

1   The tree *Salix alba* was used in the preparation of
      which drug?

2   When is hormone-replacement therapy sometimes
      used?

3   *Diabetes insipidus* affects which organ?

4   Which disease, targeted by the World Health
      Organization, was eradicated by 1980?

5   Malarial parasites live in which part of the mosquito?

6   Dopamine acts on which part of the body?

7   Amniocentesis is used in which field of medicine?

8   Hodgkin's disease is what type of disease?

9   The T cells of the human immune system mature in
      which gland?

10   English writer D H Lawrence died of which disease?

Answers on page 182

1   Which philosophical system was founded by the Chinese philosopher Lao Zi?

2   Which Christian theory sees Christ as freeing the poor from oppression?

3   Which 17th-century radical Christian sect was headed by Gerrard Winstanley?

4   In which religion do men take a last name meaning 'lion' and women one meaning 'princess'?

5   Which communist leader expounded the concept of permanent revolution?

6   Who founded the Jesuits?

7   What, to a Muslim, is the Kaaba?

8   What do we now call the Christian Revival Association?

9   What language did Jesus probably speak?

10   Who published his laws of planetary motion in 1609 and 1619?

Answers on page 182

1   Which scientist invented the aperture synthesis method of radio astronomy?

2   The red shift is an astronomical example of which common terrestrial phenomenon?

3   What can contract to give birth to a star?

4   What is a parsec?

5   Whose theories for ever banished the ether from science?

6   Superstrings exist in a universe of how many dimensions?

7   Which type of celestial object emits bursts of energy at regular intervals?

8   Which theory suggested that the universe had no beginning?

9   What shape is the Milky Way?

10   The energy of the Sun is produced by which kind of reaction?

Answers on page 183

1   Which early screen idol was known as 'the Profile'?

2   Native life in which part of India is the subject of Satyajit Ray's great trilogy of films beginning with *Pather Panchali*?

3   Which director's films include *Witness* and *The Mosquito Coast*?

4   Who wrote the screenplay for the Bond film *You Only Live Twice*?

5   Where is the main centre of Dutch broadcasting?

6   Which actress's first 'talkie' was *Anna Christie*?

7   Which Hollywood legend's career spanned *Way Down East* in 1920 and *The Whales of August* in 1987?

8   Which 1971 film won Jane Fonda the first of her Oscars?

9   Which American playwright wrote the television film *Playing For Time* in 1980?

10   What was Sam Goldwyn's real name?

Answers on page 183

1   What is the name of a bass xylophone?

2   In which Italian town did the violin-makers Stradivari and Amati ply their craft?

3   Which was Richard Wagner's last opera?

4   Where was Handel's *Messiah* first performed?

5   Which American composer wrote the march 'Stars and Stripes Forever!' and invented a bass tuba?

6   What did Cecil Sharp collect?

7   Which modern composer composed the operas *Punch and Judy*, *The Mask of Orpheus*, and *Gawain*?

8   Which useful musical device was invented by Johann Maelzel in 1814?

9   Who composed *Danse macabre* and *Carnival of the Animals*?

10   What kind of songs did Charles Wesley write?

Answers on page 183

1 Who first proposed that the geological processes occurring now can be used to understand the changes of the past?

2 Who proposed that in searching for an explanation one should reduce assumptions to a minimum?

3 Which philosopher of science made popular the term 'paradigm'?

4 Who developed a general electrochemical theory as well as effective ways of poisoning people?

5 Which branch of philosophy emphasizes the importance of sense experience?

6 Which branch of philosophy rejects as meaningless everything except logic, mathematics, science, and observation?

7 Who claimed that the sciences and the arts were divided by a gaping chasm?

8 Which philosopher of science wrote *Against Method*?

9 Who said 'the physicists have known sin; and this is a knowledge which they cannot lose'?

10 Which problem ensures that no scientific statement can ever be 'true'?

Answers on page 183

1   Which of Eugene O'Neill's plays was first seen 15 years after it was written and after he had died?

2   Who is the actor thought to have first played the parts of Hamlet, King Lear, and Othello?

3   Which Oscar-winning actor starred in the 1984 Broadway revival of *Death of a Salesman*?

4   On which real-life person was Terence Rattigan's *Ross* based?

5   Around the altar of which god were the earliest Greek dramas performed?

6   Which monarch protected Molière from attacks caused by his satires?

7   Who wrote the music for Bertolt Brecht's *The Threepenny Opera*?

8   In which other field did the playwright John Vanbrugh make his mark?

9   The brother of which British prime minister wrote *Lloyd George Knew My Father* and *The Chiltern Hundreds*?

10   What is the name of the title character in *The Merchant of Venice*?

Answers on page 183

1 Who erected the Taj Mahal in memory of his favourite wife?

2 Who was joint architect with Vanbrugh at Castle Howard and Blenheim Palace?

3 Which Parisian church contains the remains of Napoleon?

4 Which New York museum did Frank Lloyd Wright build in 1959?

5 In which city is the world's largest medieval cathedral to be found?

6 Which countries are linked by the Karakoram Highway, completed in 1979?

7 In which American state is the 'planet in a bottle' test project, BioSphere 2?

8 What is the British monarch's official Scottish residence?

9 Which Venetian building is linked to the Doge's Palace by the Bridge of Sighs?

10 On which river is the Kariba dam?

Answers on page 184

1   Who owned the Indian chemical plant whose leak accident caused the deaths of 2,600 citizens of Bhopal?

2   Which gas, produced in the guts of ruminant mammals, makes a constantly increasing contribution to global warming?

3   Which organization coordinates the prices of oil exports from Middle-East and Third-World countries?

4   Myxomatosis kills rabbits by infecting them with which kind of microbe?

5   The quagga became extinct in the 1880's. What was it?

6   Who is the patron saint of ecologists?

7   Who did Chico Mendes represent in the forests of Brazil?

8   Which type of oryx has been successfully reintroduced to the wild?

9   The *Exxon Valdez* polluted the coastline of which US state?

10   Leaded petrol contains an additive consisting of tetraethyl lead and which other compound?

Answers on page 184

1   Who was the first English woman to qualify in medicine?

2   Where were 153 Sioux massacred by the US army two weeks after Sitting Bull was killed?

3   What is Bora-Bora?

4   Who co-wrote the *Liverpool Oratorio* with Carl Davis in 1991?

5   What is the least spoken official language in Switzerland?

6   Where did Livingstone and Stanley meet in 1871?

7   Who translated the Greek New Testament in 1516 and exposed the Vulgate as a second-hand document?

8   What is the capital of Sardinia?

9   Where was the treaty signed which ended the Crimean War?

10 Who painted *The Awakening Conscience* and *The Light of the World*?

Answers on page 184

1   Which is the oldest colonial city in the Americas, founded by Christopher Columbus's brother?

2   In which country did the Tupamaros urban guerrilla movement operate?

3   What is the name of the Barbadian dialect of English?

4   Who was the left-wing president of Chile who was killed during a coup by the army in 1973?

5   Which extinct volcano in the Andes is the highest mountain in the Americas?

6   What nationality was the composer Heitor Villa-Lobos?

7   Which two Central American countries fought the 'soccer war' in 1969?

8   What are Peru's two official languages?

9   What colour is the middle stripe on the Argentine flag?

10   What is the meaning of the Indian word *Amossona*, which gives the River Amazon its name?

Answers on page 184

1   Which is the dominant generation in the ferns?

2   Which step in photosynthesis is responsible for splitting water molecules?

3   What is the main use of the tree *Citrus bergamia*?

4   Which is the biggest flower in the world?

5   Machiavelli used which plant's name as the title of one of his books?

6   Which physician developed a type of remedy involving wild flowers?

7   Aphids insert their mouthparts into which part of a plant?

8   What kind of an organism causes a 'rust' attack on plants?

9   The best longbows were constructed from which wood?

10   Which beautiful youth from mythology has a plant named after him?

Answers on page 185

1   Who directed the 1963 film *The Leopard*?

2   Who wrote the 1974 thriller *The Dogs of War*?

3   Which cartoon cat was the first to make the crossing from screen to comic strip?

4   What group of British political campaigners were affected by the Cat and Mouse Act?

5   Who collaborated with Christopher Isherwood on the verse drama *The Dog Beneath the Skin*?

6   Which make of car is built at Wolfsburg?

7   Who was called 'the Lion of Judah'?

8   Which size of poodle comes between standard and toy?

9   Which dog's name means 'badger-dog' in German?

10   Which jazzman recorded *Bitches' Brew* in 1970?

Answers on page 185

1   Who was the British minister of health who introduced the National Health Service?

2   In which war was the battle of Ramillies?

3   Which people did Alaric lead in the capture of Rome in 410?

4   Which French revolutionary was nicknamed 'the Incorruptible'?

5   Where did George Washington's army endure the winter of 1777–78?

6   In which country is the castle that gives the Habsburg dynasty its name?

7   Whom did Charles V confront at the Diet of Worms in 1521?

8   Which battle of 1746 ended the Jacobite revolution?

9   Who was appointed successor to Hitler in 1939 but expelled from the Nazi party six years later?

10   Who was the first democratically elected Marxist head of state?

Answers on page 185

1   In Greek mythology, which god was the twin brother of Artemis?

2   Which British occultist designed a tarot pack that bears his name?

3   Whose collection of fairy tales published in 1697 included 'Little Red Riding Hood' and 'Sleeping Beauty'?

4   Who wrote the Arthurian romance *Le Morte d'Arthur*?

5   How were the goddesses Aglaia, Euphrosyne, and Thalia collectively known?

6   Which Massachusetts town was the scene of witch trials in 1692 which led to 19 executions?

7   When is Walpurgis Night, noted for witches' sabbaths?

8   Which British writer, noted for a series of novels dealing with black magic and occultism, also wrote *Murder off Miami*?

9   Who in Greek mythology was seduced by Zeus disguised as a swan?

10   In the mythology of which ancient people was Marduk the creator of Earth and humans?

Answers on page 185

1   Which language is spoken by about one-third of Algerians and nearly two-thirds of Moroccans?

2   Who was Peter Abelard's secret lover?

3   The holder of which office is responsible for organizing major British state occasions?

4   Who was the unsuccessful Democratic candidate for the US presidency in both 1952 and 1956?

5   In which of the arts has Richard Avedon distinguished himself?

6   What was Lewis Carroll's hobby?

7   In which city was Maria Callas born?

8   What was the real first name of the couturier Coco Chanel?

9   What pen name was used by the Spanish orator Dolores Ibarruri, who said 'It is better to die on your feet than to live on your knees'?

10   Who stated that populations increase in geometric ratio and food only in arithmetic ratio?

Answers on page 185

1   What is the two-wheeled vehicle pulled in harness racing called?

2   Which make of car won the Le Mans 24 Hour race five times between 1951 and 1958?

3   Who invented pneumatic tyres in 1888?

4   Where were the first passenger trams introduced in 1832?

5   What was Ford's first car?

6   Which places were connected by the first public steam railway?

7   With which race team did James Hunt begin his Formula 1 career?

8   In which country was the first speed of more than 100 mph recorded for a car?

9   Which company made the first mass-produced car with four-wheel steering?

10   Which company took over Bugatti after its founder's death in 1947?

Answers on page 185

ANSWERS

Answers to the questions in this book are followed by an entry in brackets. This shows where you can look up the answer in *The Hutchinson Encyclopedia* (1995 edition) and find further information.

1   General Knowledge

1. New York (United Nations)
2. *Spycatcher* (*Spycatcher*)
3. Hill figures (hill figure)
4. *Schindler's List* (Academy Awards – panel)
5. Footpad (footpad)
6. Michael Heseltine (Heseltine)
7. Independence Day (Independence Day)
8. Michaelangelo (Michaelangelo)
9. Rupert Murdoch (Murdoch)
10. Milky Way (Milky Way)

2   History of Science

1. Isaac Newton (Newton)
2. Albert Einstein (relativity)
3. Copernicus (Copernicus)
4. Charles Darwin (Darwin)
5. Galileo (Galileo)
6. Watson (Watson)
7. Michael Faraday (Faraday)
8. Pavlov (conditioning)
9. New Zealand (Rutherford)
10. Galilei (Galileo)

3   Africa

1. Southern Rhodesia, now Zimbabwe (Zimbabwe)
2. Green (Libya – panel)
3. Burkina Faso (Burkina Faso)
4. Tutankhamen (Tutankhamen)
5. Sadat (Sadat)
6. Kenya (inside front cover)
7. Kilimanjaro (Kilimanjaro)
8. David Livingstone (Stanley)
9. Blue and White (Nile)
10. Congo (Congo – panel)

4   Science Miscellany

1. Decibel (decibel)
2. Arachnids (arachnid)
3. Electron (electron)
4. Joule (joule)
5. Acoustics (acoustics)
6. Halogens (halogen)
7. Nucleus (DNA)
8. Evaporation (evaporation)
9. Reptile (iguana; lizard)
10. Nicolaus Copernicus (Copernicus)

5   Colours

1. Legs (redshank)
2. Mercury (mercury)
3. Rice (rice – caption)
4. White (France – panel)
5. The White Rabbit (*Alice's Adventures in Wonderland*)
6. Pink Floyd (Pink Floyd)
7. Johann Strauss (Strauss)
8. Beatles (Beatles)
9. Suez Canal (Suez Canal)
10. Denmark (Greenland)

6   Senses

1. The retina (retina)
2. Beethoven (Beethoven)
3. Optic nerve (eye)
4. Echolocation (echolocation)
5. Iris (iris)
6. Pupil (eye)
7. Cones (eye – caption)
8. Tinnitus (tinnitus)
9. Four (taste)
10. Ossicles (ear)

7   Water, Water, Everywhere

1 H$_2$O (water)
2 Rabies (rabies)
3 Pacific (Pacific)
4 Handel (Handel)
5 To help prevent tooth decay (fluoridation)
6 Aquarius (Aquarius)
7 Richard Nixon (Nixon)
8 *Babies* (Kingsley)
9 Tributaries (river)
10 Narcissus (Narcissus)

8   Kings and Queens

1 Six (George)
2 Tudor (Tudor dynasty)
3 Juan Carlos (Juan Carlos)
4 William II (William II)
5 First century BC (Cleopatra)
6 The Sun King (Louis XIV)
7 Anne Boleyn (Elizabeth I)
8 Greece (Greece)
9 Henry V (Henry V)
10 Lear (*King Lear*)

9   Time

1 3,600 (second)
2 Sundial (sundial)
3 Quartz (quartz)
4 Atomic clocks (clock)
5 Six (time)
6 Greenwich (Greenwich)
7 HG Wells (Wells)
8 Metronome (metronome)
9 Second (second)
10 Milan (clock)

10   Popular Music

1 Gene Kelly (Kelly)
2 Cliff Richard (Richard)
3 Beach Boys (Beach Boys)
4 Paul Simon (Simon)
5 Who (Who, the)
6 Glenn Miller (Miller)
7 Otis Redding (Redding)
8 Prince (Prince)
9 Barbra Streisand (Streisand)
10 Sex Pistols (Sex Pistols)

11   General Knowledge

1 Flute (Galway)
2 Short tennis (short tennis)
3 Shark (shark)
4 Brain (cerebral)
5 Potato (potato)
6 Aldous Huxley (Huxley)
7 Actors (Equity)
8 The Chancellor of the Exchequer (Downing Street)
9 St Christopher (Christopher, St)
10 Black Sea (Black Sea – map)

12   Animal Kingdom

1 Omnivores (omnivore)
2 9 feet (giraffe)
3 To absorb oxygen (gill)
4 An American monkey (marmoset)
5 Cheetah (cheetah)
6 Bamboo shoots (panda)
7 Ornithology (ornithology)
8 An ostrich (ostrich – caption)
9 Octopus (octopus)
10 A lizard (gecko)

13 Asia

1 Persia (Iran)
2 India (India – panel)
3 Islamabad (Pakistan – panel)
4 Miniature trees (bonsai)
5 Genghis Khan (Genghis Khan)
6 China (Gang of Four)
7 Soya (soya bean)
8 Jordan (Jordan)
9 New Guinea (islands – panel)
10 Red (Japan – panel)

14 Human Body

1 Shoulder blade (scapula)
2 Patella (human body)
3 Hypothalamus (hypothalamus)
4 Stomach (stomach)
5 Brain (cranium)
6 Pancreas (pancreas)
7 Diaphragm (human body)
8 Kidney (kidney)
9 The neck (thyroid)
10 Coccyx (human body)

15 Comedians and Clowns

1 *Monty Python's Flying Circus*
  (*Monty Python's Flying Circus*)
2 *Hancock's Half Hour* (Hancock)
3 *Sesame Street* (Henson)
4 *Fantasia* (Disney)
5 Bob Hope and Bing Crosby
  (Crosby)
6 Gauls (Astérix the Gaul)
7 Three (Jerome)
8 Dudley Moore (Moore)
9 'What's up, Doc?' (Bugs Bunny)
10 Judy (Punch)

16 Solar System

1 The Sun (solar system)
2 Mercury and Venus (planets)
3 Venus (Venus)
4 Uranus (Uranus)
5 A comet (Halley's comet)
6 Venus (Venus)
7 11 (sunspot)
8 moon (satellite)
9 Pluto (Pluto)
10 9 (solar system)

17 Literature

1 Richmal Crompton (Crompton)
2 Ernest Hemingway (Hemingway)
3 *The Pilgrim's Progress* (Bunyan)
4 *Black Beauty* (Sewell)
5 Rabbits (Adams)
6 Captain Ahab (*Moby-Dick*)
7 *Verona* (Shakespeare)
8 Chocolate (Dahl)
9 Twenty thousand leagues (Verne)
10 Narnia (Lewis)

18 Transport

1 *Titanic* (Titanic)
2 Magnetic (maglev)
3 Concorde (Concorde)
4 Saturn V (Saturn rocket)
5 English Channel (*Gossamer
  Albatross*)
6 TGV (TGV)
7 Audi Quattro (car – panel)
8 HMS *Beagle* (Darwin)
9 Trireme (trireme)
10 A bicycle (bicycle)

19 Sports and Games

1 Paul Gascoigne (Gascoigne)
2 Sumo (sumo wrestling)
3 Deuce (tennis, lawn)
4 Ryder Cup (Ryder Cup)
5 Six (football, American)
6 Fairway (golf)
7 Cricket (cricket)
8 Carl Lewis (Lewis)
9 Surfing (Beach Boys, the)
10 Gymnastics (gymnastics)

20 People

1 The Red Baron (Richthofen)
2 Classifying books (Dewey)
3 Dr Watson (Doyle)
4 John Paul I (John Paul I)
5 Maoris (Maori)
6 Elvis Presley (Presley – caption)
7 Census (census)
8 Benjamin Franklin (Franklin)
9 Grace Kelly (Kelly)
10 Walter Raleigh (Raleigh – caption)

21 General Knowledge

1 Gymnastics (gymnastics)
2 Seven (netball)
3 The Pope (encyclical)
4 J S Bach (Bach)
5 William Caxton (Caxton; printing)
6 Delilah (Samson)
7 Vesuvius (Pompeii)
8 Isosceles (triangle – diagram)
9 Spanish (Domingo)
10 Octave (octave)

22 Earth

1 Nitrogen (nitrogen)
2 Molten iron and nickel (Earth)
3 Assam (Himalayas)
4 Coal (coal)
5 Pacific (Pacific Ocean)
6 Lava (lava)
7 20% (oxygen)
8 Synoptic (weather)
9 Tsunami (tsunami)
10 A river (river – caption)

23 Australasia

1 A politician (Melbourne)
2 Tasmania (Australia – map)
3 1956 (Olympic Games – panel)
4 *Waltzing Matilda* (Paterson, Banjo)
5 Butterfly (butterfly)
6 Coral Sea (Coral Sea)
7 Western Australia (Western Australia)
8 The Tropic of Capricorn (Australia – map)
9 To watch an eclipse (Cook, James)
10 Crime (Marsh, Ngaio)

24 Material World

1 Lignite (lignite)
2 Sand (glass)
3 Graphite (graphite)
4 Lanolin (lanolin)
5 Collagen (tendon)
6 Cellulose (cellulose)
7 Teflon (Teflon)
8 Enamel (tooth – caption)
9 Iron (iron)
10 Cast iron (cast iron)

25   Europe

1 Bonn (Bonn)
2 Majorca (Majorca)
3 Danube (Budapest)
4 Switzerland and Austria (Liechtenstein)
5 Denmark (Denmark – panel)
6 Portugal (Brazil)
7 Loire (Loire)
8 Switzerland (Switzerland)
9 Copenhagen (Copenhagen)
10 Munich (Chamberlain)

26   Technology

1 Distributor (distributor)
2 Fibre optics (fibre optics)
3 Transformer (transformer)
4 Flywheel (flywheel)
5 Transfusion (transfusion)
6 Frequency Modulation (FM)
7 Amplifier (amplifier)
8 Clutch (clutch)
9 Aerodynamics (aerodynamics)
10 Pasteurization (pasteurization)

27   Partners

1 Eleanor (Roosevelt)
2 Oliver Hardy (Laurel and Hardy)
3 Marie Antoinette (Marie Antoinette)
4 Ballooning (Montgolfier)
5 Desdemona (*Othello*)
6 Castor and Pollux/Polydeuces (Castor and Pollux/Polydeuces)
7 Mr Hyde (Stevenson)
8 Romulus and Remus (Romulus)
9 Jeeves (Wodehouse)
10 Cain and Abel (Abel)

28   Murders and Assassinations

1 John F Kennedy (Kennedy)
2 Christopher Marlowe (Marlowe)
3 Sweden (Palme)
4 Jack the Ripper (Jack the Ripper)
5 Al Capone (St Valentine's Day Massacre)
6 Agatha Christie (Christie)
7 John Lennon (Lennon)
8 Hamlet (*Hamlet*)
9 Guillotine (guillotine)
10 Sarajevo (Franz Ferdinand; Sarajevo)

29   Politics

1 Jimmy Carter (Carter)
2 Cambodia (Pol Pot)
3 Mussolini (Mussolini)
4 Elysée Palace (Elysée Palace)
5 Israel (Israel)
6 Conservative (Conservative Party)
7 Amnesty International (Amnesty International)
8 Adolf Hitler (Hitler)
9 Drug trafficking (Noriega)
10 Every four years (United States of America)

30 Visual Arts

1 Sydney Opera House (Sydney – caption)
2 Andy Warhol (Warhol)
3 *The Laughing Cavalier* (Hals)
4 Impressionism (Impressionism)
5 Michaelangelo (Michaelangelo – picture)
6 Faces of four presidents (Borglum)
7 Brighton (Brighton)
8 Seventeenth (Rembrandt)
9 Henry VIII (Holbein)
10 Vinci (Leonardo da Vinci)

31 General Knowledge

1 Thomas Edison (Edison)
2 Bridge (bridge)
3 English Civil War (Civil War, English)
4 Spaniel (spaniel)
5 Goat (cashmere)
6 Lockheed (Lockheed)
7 Blue (sapphire)
8 Old Bailey (Old Bailey)
9 Excessively long nose (Cyrano de Bergerac)
10 Billy Butlin (holiday camp)

32 Elements

1 Hydrogen (periodic table)
2 Chlorine (chlorine)
3 Silicon (silicon)
4 Gold (carat)
5 Zinc (brass)
6 Aluminium (aluminium)
7 Rare earth (lanthanide)
8 Gold (gold)
9 Magnesium (magnesium oxide)
10 Carbon (battery)

33 North America

1 Niagara (Niagara Falls)
2 Ottawa (Canada – panel)
3 Hollywood (Hollywood)
4 Democrat (Kennedy)
5 Oklahoma (Rodgers)
6 George Custer (Custer)
7 Montréal (Montréal)
8 Las Vegas (Las Vegas)
9 Last Frontier (Alaska)
10 Franklin D Roosevelt (Roosevelt)

34 Medicine and Health

1 Anaesthetist (anaesthetic)
2 Blood (transfusion)
3 Antibiotic (antibiotic)
4 In the 1970s (hormone-replacement therapy)
5 Alcohol (cholesterol)
6 Polyunsaturated fat (polyunsaturate)
7 Heart (pacemaker)
8 Stomach (gastroenteritis)
9 Iron (anaemia)
10 Scurvy (scurvy)

35 Beliefs and Ideas

1 Judas Iscariot (Judas Iscariot)
2 Mahatma Gandhi (Gandhi, Mohandas)
3 Hippies (hippie)
4 Hinduism (Hinduism)
5 Trampled by the King's racehorse (Davison)
6 Confucius (Confucianism)
7 Nirvana (nirvana)
8 *On the Origin of Species* (Darwin)
9 Revelation (Revelation)
10 Four (Buddhism)

36   Universe

1 Formation of the universe (Big Bang)
2 Cosmology (cosmology)
3 Hydrogen (hydrogen)
4 Nebula (nebula)
5 Distance (light year)
6 Galaxy (galaxy)
7 a) 10–20 (universe)
8 In the Earth's orbit (Hubble)
9 Orion (Orion)
10 Black holes (black hole)

37   Film and TV

1 *The Saint* (Moore)
2 Sergio Leone (Leone)
3 *A Hard Day's Night* (Beatles)
4 Sony (Videotape recorder)
5 Madonna (Madonna)
6 Steve McQueen (McQueen)
7 Holly Hunter (Academy Awards: recent winners – panel)
8 Anthony Hopkins (Hopkins)
9 Austria (Schwarzenegger)
10 Fred Quimby (Quimby)

38   Music

1 Vivaldi (Vivaldi)
2 Nine (Beethoven; Dvořák; Vaughan Williams)
3 Piano (Chopin)
4 Balalaika (balalaika)
5 Schubert (Schubert)
6 Three (brass instrument)
7 *Carmen* (Bizet)
8 Waltz (Strauss)
9 Mezzo-soprano (mezzo-soprano)
10 Violin (Kennedy)

39   On the Stage

1 Stratford-upon-Avon (Shakespeare)
2 *St Joan* (Shaw)
3 Bayreuth (Bayreuth)
4 Barry Humphries (Humphries)
5 Noël Coward (Coward)
6 Laurence Olivier (Olivier)
7 *The Boy Who Wouldn't Grow Up* (*Peter Pan*)
8 Mummers' play (Mummers' play)
9 Pantomime (pantomime)
10 Woodstock (Woodstock)

40   What's in a Name?

1 Catherine (Henry VIII)
2 Steam engine (Newcomen)
3 Ampère (ampere; Ampère)
4 Herald of Free Enterprise (manslaughter, corporate)
5 Heartsease (pansy)
6 Cassius Clay (Ali)
7 Istanbul (Istanbul)
8 Cape Canaveral (Cape Canaveral)
9 Blondin (Blondin)
10 Boomtown Rats (Geldof)

41 Environment

1 Chlorofluorocarbon (chlorofluorocarbon)
2 Rhinoceros (rhinoceros)
3 Ivory (ivory)
4 Carbon monoxide (carbon monoxide)
5 Nitrate (nitrate)
6 Nuclear testing (Greenpeace)
7 UV rays (ozone)
8 Sulphur dioxide (acid rain)
9 A catalytic converter (catalytic converter)
10 Aluminium (aluminium)

42 On Wheels

1 Fiat (Alfa Romeo)
2 Roulette (roulette)
3 Catherine (Catherine of Alexandria, St)
4 Egyptian (pottery: chronology – panel)
5 b) 300 kph/185 mph (railway – caption)
6 Brazilian (Senna)
7 Dunlop (Dunlop)
8 Two (Hansom)
9 Italy (motor racing)
10 Mini (car: chronology – panel)

43 Latin America and the Caribbean

1 Brasília (Brasília)
2 Falkland Islands (Falklands War)
3 Venezuela (Angel Falls)
4 Tobago (Trinidad and Tobago)
5 Tierra del Fuego (Tierra del Fuego)
6 Bolivia and Paraguay (inside front cover)
7 Panama (Panama)
8 Sugar Loaf mountain (Rio de Janeiro)
9 Haiti (Haiti)
10 Caribbean (Panama Canal – map)

44 Plant Kingdom

1 Bark (bark)
2 Chlorophyll (chlorophyll)
3 Citric acid (lemon – caption)
4 Carbon dioxide (photosynthesis)
5 Algae (algae)
6 Evergreen (evergreen)
7 Adam (Adam)
8 Cactus (cactus – caption)
9 Yew (yew – caption)
10 Hemlock (Socrates)

45 Cats and Dogs

1 Peter Sellers (Sellers)
2 St Bernard (St Bernard)
3 Sherlock Holmes (Doyle)
4 South America (jaguar)
5 Richard I (Richard I)
6 Erwin Rommel (Rommel)
7 July and August (Leo)
8 No tail (Man, Isle of)
9 Dalmatians (Dalmatian)
10 Tiger (tiger)

46   Colours in Science

1. Green (chlorophyll)
2. Red (haemoglobin)
3. Red (Mars)
4. Blue (Neptune)
5. Red (electromagnetic waves – diagram)
6. A plant (indigo)
7. Blue (lapis lazuli)
8. Astronomy (red shift)
9. Red (red giant)
10. Verdigris (verdigris)

47   History

1. Elephants (Hannibal)
2. Calcutta (Black Hole of Calcutta)
3. England and France (Hundred Years' War)
4. Nelson Mandela (Mandela; South Africa)
5. Greece (Troy)
6. George Washington (Washington)
7. Molotov (Molotov cocktail)
8. Mayor of London (Whittington)
9. Elba (Napoleon I)
10. Czechoslovakia (Havel)

48   Myth and Magic

1. Camelot (Camelot)
2. Pegasus (Pegasus)
3. Flute (Mozart)
4. Tom Thumb (Tom Thumb)
5. Bram Stoker (Dracula)
6. Jason (Jason)
7. Thor (Thor)
8. Macbeth (*Macbeth*)
9. October 31 (Hallowe'en)
10. Copenhagen (Andersen; Copenhagen)

49   People

1. Thomas More (More)
2. Venice (Venice)
3. William (Gladstone; Walton; Wilberforce)
4. Ballet (ballet)
5. Mormons (Mormon)
6. Philistines (Goliath)
7. Four (barbershop)
8. Charles de Gaulle (de Gaulle)
9. Samuel Johnson (Johnson – caption)
10. Hungary (Hungary – panel)

50   Who, What, Where?

1. The Pope (Vatican City State)
2. John F Kennedy (Kennedy)
3. A bell (Big Ben)
4. Francis Drake (Drake)
5. Tower of London (crown jewels)
6. Saigon (Ho Chi Minh City)
7. Mark Antony (Mark Antony)
8. Dogs (Cruft)
9. On the road to Damascus (Paul, St)
10. McDonald's (McDonald's)

51   General Knowledge

1 Romania (Transylvania)
2 Squint (squint)
3 James II (Glorious Revolution)
4 Pakistan (Jinnah – caption)
5 Orly (Orly)
6 Mars (Mars)
7 Spoonerism (spoonerism)
8 King (King)
9 Portugal (Lusitania)
10 Green (pistachio)

52   History of Science

1 Richard Owen (Owen)
2 Archimedes (Archimedes – quote)
3 A theory of evolution (Lamarck)
4 Medicine (Galen)
5 Karl Popper (Popper)
6 Atomic bomb (Oppenheimer)
7 Leibniz (Leibniz)
8 Linnaeus (Linnaeus)
9 Röntgen (Röntgen)
10 Mendelevium (mendelevium)

53   What's in a Name?

1 Edward (Black Prince)
2 Black (Black Friday, Black Thursday, Black Monday)
3 Edith (Nesbit)
4 Herbert Hoover (Hoover Dam)
5 Partisans (partisan)
6 Shelley (Shelley)
7 Rita Hayworth (Hayworth)
8 Fitzgerald (Kennedy)
9 Bomber Harris (Harris)
10 Emma Thompson (Thompson)

54   Africa

1 Morocco (Morocco)
2 Gordon (Gordon)
3 Zambia and Zimbabwe (Victoria Falls)
4 Dinar (Algeria – panel; Tunisia – panel)
5 Humphrey Bogart (Bogart)
6 Portugal (Angola)
7 Alan Paton (Paton)
8 Rastafarianism (Rastafarianism)
9 Great Rift Valley (Rift Valley, Great)
10 Bartolomeu Diaz (Diaz)

55   Science Miscellany

1 Relativity theory (relativity)
2 Nervous system (caffeine)
3 Calorimeter (calorimeter)
4 pH scale (pH)
5 Frederick Sanger (Sanger)
6 Ohm (ohm)
7 Convex lens (lens)
8 Hooke's law (Hooke's law)
9 Amino acids (amino acid)
10 Astronomy (Hubble)

56   Colours

1 The Color of Money (Academy Awards – table)
2 Orange (salmon)
3 Five (snooker – diagram)
4 Large, bright stars (red giant)
5 Nell Gwyn (Gwyn, Nell)
6 George Gershwin (Gershwin)
7 Kerry Packer (Packer, Kerry)
8 Golden Hind (Drake)
9 The Wall Street stock market crashed (Black Thursday)
10 Disneyland (Orange County)

57 Built World

1 Morocco (Casablanca)
2 Edwin Lutyens (Lutyens)
3 Uganda (dam)
4 Lighthouses (lighthouse)
5 Blackpool (Blackpool)
6 To cover scars after a fire (White House)
7 Pompidou Centre (Paris)
8 Istanbul (Istanbul)
9 arch (bridge)
10 Gothic (architecture)

58 Kings and Queens

1 Canute (Canute)
2 Punctuality (Louis XVIII – quote)
3 Belgium (Belgium)
4 Charles II (Charles II)
5 Richard III (Bosworth, Battle of)
6 Spain (Columbus)
7 Warwick (Warwick)
8 Netherlands (Netherlands)
9 Benny Goodman (Goodman)
10 Wilhelm II (Wilhelm II)

59 Popular Music

1 Jimi Hendrix (Hendrix)
2 Frank Sinatra (Sinatra)
3 Guitar (Reinhardt)
4 Johnny Cash (Cash)
5 David Bowie (Bowie – caption)
6 Billie Holiday (Holiday)
7 *Born to Run* (Springsteen)
8 Grateful Dead (Grateful Dead)
9 Richard Rodgers (Rodgers)
10 Vera Lynn (Lynn)

60 Name the Year

1 1929 (Hoover; Wall Street crash, 1929)
2 1989 (Ceausescu; Nicholson)
3 1978 (Margaret; John Paul I; John Paul II)
4 1966 (Dylan; Moore)
5 1944 (Bogart; D-day)
6 1963 (John XXIII; Kennedy; Tereshkova)
7 1991 (Gorbachev; Maxwell)
8 1936 (Edward VIII; Owens)
9 1982 (Brezhnev; Falklands War)
10 1969 (Apollo project; France – panel)

61 General Knowledge

1 Austrian (Waldheim)
2 Turkey (Ephesus)
3 Venice (Venice)
4 Joseph Goebbels (Goebbels)
5 Triathlon (triathlon)
6 Potomac (Potomac)
7 Oliver Cromwell (Cromwell)
8 Brown (mink)
9 Ash Wednesday (Ash Wednesday)
10 Jack Hobbs (Hobbs)

62 Animal Kingdom

1 Krill (krill)
2 Ganesh (Ganesh)
3 Ethology (ethology)
4 Stationary (sessile)
5 The outside (exoskeleton)
6 Skull (skull – caption)
7 It doesn't have one (gestation)
8 Arachnid (arachnid)
9 Sharks (shark – caption)
10 Crop (crop)

63   Asia

1. Vasco da Gama (Gama, Vasco da)
2. Jute (jute)
3. Malaysia (Malaysia – panel)
4. Hirohito (Hirohito)
5. Victoria (Hong Kong)
6. Scheherazade (*Arabian Nights*)
7. Egypt (Arab League)
8. Yellow Sea (Yellow Sea)
9. Amritsar (Amritsar)
10. Yemen (Yemen)

64   Human Body

1. Ureter (human body)
2. Lung (alveolus)
3. Tendon (tendon)
4. Bone marrow (bone marrow)
5. Erythrocyte (erythrocyte)
6. Liver (bile)
7. Colon (colon)
8. Atrium (heart)
9. Keratin (keratin)
10. Femur (human body)

65   Comedians and Clowns

1. Superman (Superman)
2. Alan Bennett (Bennett – quote)
3. The Goons (Sellers – caption)
4. Joseph Grimaldi (Grimaldi)
5. Stan and Oliver (Laurel and Hardy; Hardy)
6. Joe Orton (Orton)
7. Ealing (Ealing Studios)
8. George Formby (Formby)
9. Harold Lloyd (Lloyd)
10. St Trinian's (Searle)

66   Solar System

1. Earth (planets)
2. Eight (Neptune)
3. Saturn (Saturn)
4. Jupiter (Jupiter)
5. Pluto (Pluto)
6. Earth (Earth)
7. Ganymede (Jupiter)
8. Mercury (Mercury)
9. Titania (Uranus)
10. Venus (Venus)

67   Quote, Unquote

1. W C Fields (Fields – quote)
2. *Pinocchio* (Collodi – quote)
3. History (Ford – quote)
4. Queen Victoria (Victoria – quote)
5. Greta Garbo (Garbo – caption)
6. Martin Luther King (King – quote)
7. A little learning (Pope – quote)
8. Alamein (Alamein, El, Battles of – quote)
9. Alexander Graham Bell (Bell – quote)
10. Roald Dahl (Dahl – quote)

68   Senses

1. Vibrations (lateral line system)
2. Semicircular canals (ear – caption)
3. Presbyopia (presbyopia)
4. Short sight (myopia)
5. 3 (eye)
6. Glue ear (glue ear)
7. Ciliary body (eye)
8. Nose (sense organ)
9. Phytochrome (photoperiodism)
10. Touch (Venus flytrap – caption)

69	Literature

1 Wordsworth (Wordsworth)
2 Colombian (García Márquez)
3 Six (Pirandello)
4 P G Wodehouse (Wodehouse)
5 *The Picture of Dorian Gray* (Wilde)
6 Umberto Eco (Eco)
7 Norwegian (Ibsen)
8 Don Quixote (*Don Quixote de la Mancha*)
9 Geoffrey Chaucer (Chaucer)
10 George Bernard Shaw (Shaw)

70	Sports and Games

1 Diego Maradona (Maradona)
2 Boris Becker (Becker)
3 Nine (baseball)
4 Stirling Moss (Moss)
5 Joe Louis (Louis)
6 Bjorn Borg (Borg)
7 McLaren (McLaren)
8 Dressage (dressage)
9 USA (horse racing)
10 Spinners (angling)

71	General Knowledge

1 Fiction (Booker Prize for Fiction)
2 Brazil (bossa nova)
3 Thursday (Ascension Day)
4 Herring (sardine)
5 Smallpox (Jenner)
6 Croesus (Croesus)
7 Apollo (Colossus of Rhodes; Apollo of Rhodes)
8 Islam (hajj)
9 Denmark and Sweden (Kattegat)
10 Orange (black box)

72	Earth

1 Igneous (rock)
2 40,000 km (Earth)
3 Seismology (earthquake)
4 Silica (quartz)
5 Mohs' scale (Mohs' scale)
6 Carbon dioxide (greenhouse effect)
7 Nitrogen (nitrogen cycle)
8 Atmospheric pressure (barometer)
9 Movement of continental plates (tectonics)
10 Latitude (latitude)

73	Australasia

1 Errol Flynn (Flynn, Errol)
2 Robert Menzies (Menzies, Robert)
3 A marsupial (bandicoot)
4 Four times (Laver, Rodney)
5 Van Diemen's Land (Tasman)
6 Land of the long white cloud (Maori)
7 Ernest Rutherford (Rutherford, Ernest)
8 Oval (football, Australian Rules)
9 Joan Sutherland (Sutherland, Joan)
10 Nullarbor Plain (Nullarbor Plain)

74	Material World

1 Nylon (nylon)
2 Lignin (lignin)
3 Calcium carbonate (limestone)
4 Methane (natural gas)
5 Silicon (silica)
6 Cartilage (cartilage)
7 Leather (leather)
8 Gold (Midas)
9 Chromium (steel)
10 Silver (photography)

1 Malta (Malta – panel)
2 Strasbourg (Strasbourg)
3 Red and white (Denmark – panel)
4 Gdansk (Poland)
5 Milan (Milan)
6 Andalusia (Andalusia)
7 Germany (Bulgaria)
8 Czechoslovakia (Czechoslovakia)
9 Denmark (Iceland – panel)
10 Rome (Rome, Treaties of)

1 Steel (tempering)
2 Clock (pendulum)
3 Bimetallic strip (bimetallic strip)
4 Kidney machine (dialysis)
5 Genetic engineering (transgenic organism)
6 Electromagnetic effect (solenoid)
7 Loom (weaving)
8 Amplitude Modulation (AM)
9 A particle accelerator (cyclotron)
10 Differential (differential)

1 Taking a bath (Corday)
2 Ice pick (Trotsky)
3 Rajiv Gandhi (Gandhi)
4 Philippines (Aquino)
5 Russia (Nicholas II – caption)
6 Edgar Allan Poe (Poe)
7 Adam (Cain)
8 Adolf Hitler (Stauffenberg)
9 James I (Fawkes; Gunpowder Plot)
10 Actor (Booth)

1 Charles Babbage (Babbage)
2 Byte (byte)
3 RAM (memory)
4 Alan Turing (Turing)
5 Neural networks (neural network)
6 RSI (repetitive strain injury)
7 WYSIWYG (WYSIWYG)
8 William Gibson (cyberspace)
9 Machine code (interpreter)
10 1990 (computer – panel)

1 Robert Peel (Peel)
2 Charles de Gaulle (de Gaulle – caption)
3 National Party (de Klerk)
4 1990 (Hussein)
5 Dan Quayle (Quayle)
6 Dáil éireann/the Dáil (Ireland, Republic of)
7 Chancellor of the Exchequer (Churchill)
8 Francis Bacon (Bacon)
9 Portugal (Soares)
10 Yalta (Yalta Conference)

1 Turner (Turner – text and picture)
2 One (Gogh – caption)
3 Louvre (Louvre – picture)
4 Spanish (Goya)
5 Fresco (fresco)
6 John Betjeman (Betjeman)
7 Gauguin (Gauguin)
8 He took the first photograph (Niepce)
9 Picasso (Picasso)
10 Barcelona (Gaudí)

1. Maserati (Maserati)
2. Force 12 or more (hurricane)
3. Musical instrument (hurdy-gurdy)
4. 64 (draughts)
5. Sternum (sternum)
6. Magnitude of earthquakes (Richter scale)
7. Earl of Essex (Elizabeth 1)
8. Aeneas (*Aeneid*)
9. Los Angeles (Olympic venues – panel)
10. Crow (jay)

1. Phosphorus (phosphorus)
2. Aluminium (Alzheimer's disease)
3. Radon (radon)
4. Helium (helium)
5. Fluorine (fluorine)
6. Aluminium (aluminium)
7. Tin (bronze)
8. Sulphur (sulphur)
9. Zinc (zinc)
10. Fluorine (fluoridation; fluoride)

1. St Lawrence (Thousand Islands)
2. Philadelphia (Philadelphia)
3. Arizona (United States of America – map)
4. James Wolfe (Canada: history – panel; Wolfe)
5. Pierre Trudeau (Canada: prime ministers – panel)
6. Orville and Wilbur Wright (Wright)
7. Sandwich Islands (Hawaii)
8. Watching a play (Lincoln)
9. California (Yosemite)
10. Québec (Canada: provinces – panel)

1. Quinine (quinine)
2. Blood vessel (embolism)
3. Nervous system (multiple sclerosis)
4. Heart (beta-blocker)
5. Skeleton (osteoporosis)
6. Vitamin B1 (beriberi)
7. Pancreas (diabetes)
8. Swallowing (barium)
9. Virus (interferon)
10. Infertility (in vitro fertilization)

85   Beliefs and Ideas

1   Socrates (Socrates; Socratic method)
2   Epiphany (Epiphany)
3   Ayatollah (Khomeini – caption)
4   Copernicus (Copernicus – quote)
5   Six (*I Ching*)
6   Ethiopia (Rastafarianism)
7   Beatification (canonization)
8   Nineteenth (papal infallibility)
9   Hirohito (Shinto)
10   Karma (karma)

86   Universe

1   Gravitational force (gravity)
2   The expansion of the universe (red shift)
3   Sirius (Sirius)
4   Great density (neutron star)
5   Ether (ether)
6   Supernova (supernova)
7   Andromeda galaxy (Andromeda galaxy)
8   A red supergiant (Betelgeuse)
9   Helium (helium)
10   Fred Hoyle (Hoyle)

87   Film and TV

1   Felix the Cat (Sullivan)
2   Tony Curtis (Curtis)
3   *Yentl* (Streisand)
4   Cary Grant (Grant – caption)
5   *The Last Emperor* (Bertolucci)
6   Cuban (Ball)
7   *Dr No* (Connery)
8   For leaving her husband to have another man's child (Bergman)
9   Alan Bennett (Bennett)
10   David Bowie (Bowie)

88   Modern Scientists

1   Linus Pauling (Pauling)
2   Rosalind Franklin (Franklin)
3   Leo Szilard (Szilard)
4   James Chadwick (neutron)
5   Marie Curie (Curie)
6   Princeton (Einstein)
7   Quantum mechanics (Heisenberg)
8   Punctuated equilibrium (Gould)
9   Superconductivity (Kamerlingh-Onnes)
10   Fred Hoyle (Hoyle)

89   Music

1   Simon Rattle (Rattle)
2   Piano (piano)
3   Finnish (Sibelius)
4   Prokofiev (Prokofiev)
5   Thomas Beecham (Beecham – quote)
6   Mendelssohn (Mendelssohn)
7   Ralph Vaughan Williams (Vaughan Williams)
8   *The Barber of Seville* (Beaumarchais)
9   Beethoven (Beethoven)
10   Debussy (Debussy)

90   On the Stage

1   The Rose (Rose Theatre)
2   Ivor Novello (Novello)
3   *Patience* (Wilde – picture caption)
4   Rochdale (Rochdale)
5   Stephen Sondheim (Sondheim)
6   David Garrick (Garrick)
7   *Showboat* (Kern)
8   J B Priestley (Priestley)
9   The Great White Way (Broadway)
10   Sam Shepard (Shepard)

91   On Wheels

1 Silver Ghost (Rolls-Royce)
2 Rocket (railway)
3 Archaeology (Wheeler)
4 Running and swimming (triathlon)
5 Karl Benz (Benz)
6 Cowley (Nuffield)
7 Tourist Trophy (Man, Isle of)
8 Citroën (Citroën)
9 Milk Race (cycling)
10 Beetle (Porsche)

92   Environment

1 Montréal (Montréal Protocol)
2 Ukraine (Chernobyl)
3 A bloom (bloom)
4 Bhopal (Bhopal)
5 Agent Orange (Dioxin)
6 Great Barrier Reef (Great Barrier Reef)
7 On or near the equator (rainforest)
8 James Lovelock (Gaia hypothesis)
9 The trade in endangered species (CITES)
10 Mauritius (dodo)

93   Latin America and the Caribbean

1 Simon Bolívar (Bolívar)
2 Shining Path (Sendero Luminoso)
3 Netherlands (Surinam)
4 Dominican Republic (Dominican Republic)
5 Bolivia and Peru (Titicaca)
6 Colombia (Medellín)
7 Actress (Perón)
8 Bay of Pigs (Bay of Pigs)
9 Argentina (Guevara)
10 Guatemala City (Guatemala – panel)

94   Plant Kingdom

1 Phloem (phloem)
2 Bryophyta (plant classification)
3 Mesophyll (mesophyll)
4 Chloroplast (chloroplast)
5 Leaf (leaf – caption)
6 Ginkgo (ginkgo)
7 Gymnosperms (gymnosperm)
8 Root (valerian)
9 Stomata (stoma)
10 Lenticels (lenticel)

95   Cats and Dogs

1 Four (tooth)
2 Puma (puma)
3 Jane Fonda (Fonda)
4 Chihuahua (chihuahua)
5 Charles Darwin (Darwin)
6 Pit bull terrier (pit bull terrier)
7 Andrew Lloyd Webber (Lloyd Webber)
8 Earth (fox)
9 Lion (Stubbs)
10 Three (Cerberus)

96   Great Experiments

1 That the ether does not exist (Michelson)
2 The expansion of the universe (Hubble)
3 Fermi Laboratory (Fermilab)
4 Manhattan Project (Manhattan Project)
5 Four years (gene therapy)
6 Empedocles (Empedocles)
7 Archimedes (Archimedes)
8 Vesalius (Vesalius)
9 Stephen Hales (Hales)
10 Newton (light)

1 1816 (Easter Rising)
2 Medici (Medici)
3 James 1 (James I)
4 Holy Roman Emperor (Charlemagne)
5 Jamestown (Jamestown)
6 Mao Zedong (China – panel)
7 France (Panama Canal)
8 Spinning cotton (Arkwright)
9 Jomo Kenyatta (Kenyatta)
10 France (Louisiana Purchase)

98   Myth and Magic

1 Carefully targeted drugs (magic bullet)
2 Eurydice (Eurydice)
3 Capricorn (Capricornus)
4 Jackal (Anubis)
5 Cyclops (Cyclops)
6 Libra (Libra)
7 Elizabeth I (*Faerie Queene, The*)
8 Rhine (Lorelei)
9 Cassandra (Cassandra)
10 *The Rime of the Ancient Mariner* (*Ancient Mariner, the Rime of the*)

1 *Mary Rose* (*Mary Rose*)
2 New Zealand (waterfall – panel)
3 Brussels (Waterloo)
4 60–70% (water)
5 Richard Adams (Adams)
6 Colombia (Colombia – panel)
7 Fourteen (water polo)
8 Narwhal (narwhal)
9 Crystal glass (Waterford)
10 Huron (lakes – panel)

100   People

1 Catherine of Aragon (Henry VIII)
2 Karl Dönitz (Dönitz)
3 Martin Luther King (King)
4 Joe McCarthy (McCarthy)
5 Johnson (Johnson)
6 James Watt (Boulton)
7 Ireland (de Valera)
8 Dutch (Mata Hari)
9 Cars (Austin)
10 Strangled when her scarf caught in a wheel (Duncan)

101　　General Knowledge

1　Spreadsheet (spreadsheet)
2　John Glenn (Glenn)
3　Islam (five pillars of Islam)
4　Kidney (kidney – diagram)
5　Lambada (lambada)
6　Small desert fox (fennec)
7　Manet (Manet – caption)
8　East Sussex (Piltdown man)
9　D (semaphore – panel)
10　The Gambia (Gambia, The)

102　　History of Science

1　A physicist (uncertainty
　　principle)
2　Geology (uniformitarianism)
3　Padua (Harvey)
4　Wegener (Wegener)
5　California (Livermore Valley)
6　Wilhelm Reich (Reich)
7　Antoine Lavoisier (oxygen)
8　Robert Brown (Brown)
9　Mass spectrometer (Aston)
10　Edwin Hubble (Hubble)

103　　What's in a Name?

1　A mineral (fluorite)
2　Mistinguett (Mistinguett)
3　Klapka (Jerome)
4　*Thrust 2* (*Thrust 2*)
5　Uranus (Uranus; *Midsummer
　　Night's Dream, A*)
6　Umberto Eco (Eco)
7　*Vostok I* (Gagarin)
8　Grampus (grampus)
9　Switch-hitter (Mantle)
10　John Wayne (Wayne – caption)

104　　Africa

1　Nigeria (Nigeria – panel)
2　James Monroe (Monrovia)
3　Sharpeville (Sharpeville)
4　Niger (Niger – panel)
5　Egypt (Sudan)
6　Kalahari (Bushman)
7　A letter R (Rwanda – panel)
8　Tunisia (Carthage)
9　Cairo (Cairo)
10　Albert Luthuli (Luthuli)

105　　Science Miscellany

1　Cryogenics (cryogenics)
2　Hans Oersted (Oersted)
3　Chitin (chitin)
4　Aluminium (corundum)
5　Inside a cell (Golgi)
6　A type of reproduction among
　　flowering plants (ornithophily)
7　2 (Mars)
8　Ontogeny (ontogeny)
9　Alkali metals (potassium)
10　The potato (potato)

106　　Colours

1　Nathaniel Hawthorne
　　(Hawthorne, Nathaniel)
2　Selborne (White, Gilbert)
3　Rugby (Arnold, Thomas)
4　Silver (photography)
5　Insect (metamorphosis – caption)
6　Red (Garibaldi)
7　William II (William II)
8　Arthur Bliss (Bliss)
9　Scale insect (cochineal)
10　Duke of Gloucester (Elizabeth II
　　– panel)

107 Science Controversies

1 Alfred Russel Wallace (Wallace)
2 Robert Oppenheimer
   (Oppenheimer)
3 Cold fusion (cold fusion)
4 Francis Galton (eugenics)
5 Phrenology (phrenology)
6 Cyril Burt (Burt)
7 Karl Popper (Popper)
8 Alfred Wegener (Wegener)
9 Linus Pauling (Pauling)
10 Trofim Lysenko (Lysenko)

108   Kings and Queens

1 Albania (Albania)
2 Isle of Wight (Victoria)
3 Bohemia (Wenceslas)
4 Scrofula (king's evil)
5 Charles (Charles)
6 Caroline of Brunswick (Caroline
   of Brunswick)
7 Habsburg or Hapsburg
   (Habsburg)
8 Ptolemy (Ptolemy I)
9 Romania (Romania; Michael)
10 Mercia (Offa)

109   Popular Music

1 Harry (Crosby)
2 Bob Marley (Marley)
3 Sun (Cash; Presley)
4 Rolling Stones (Rolling Stones)
5 Ennio Morricone (Morricone)
6 Bananarama (Bananarama)
7 Yesterday (Beatles)
8 Texas (Texas)
9 Miles Davis (Davis)
10 MC Hammer (Hammer)

110   Name the Year

1 1957 (Macmillan; Sputnik)
2 1912 (*Titanic*; Scott)
3 1985 (*Titanic*; Greenpeace)
4 1949 (Berlin blockade; Mao
   Zedong)
5 1974 (Nixon; Stoppard)
6 1959 (Castro; Holly)
7 1975 (Ashe; Thatcher)
8 1933 (Hitler; Prohibition)
9 1965 (Leonov; Rolling Stones,
   the)
10 1980 (Borg; Carter)

111   General Knowledge

1 HIV (Gallo)
2 Money (tea)
3 Walter Raleigh (Shakespeare)
4 Roland (Rowland)
5 A musical instrument (koto)
6 William Hurt (Hurt)
7 Rowing (rowing)
8 Corfu (Corfu)
9 Christopher Fry (Fry)
10 Ernst Heinkel (Heinkel)

112   Animal Kingdom

1 A Himalayan pheasant
   (tragopan)
2 An ornithologist (petrel)
3 Protozoa (taxis)
4 Muscle tissue (myoglobin)
5 Punctuated equilibrium
   (punctuated equilibrium model)
6 Archaeopteryx (archaeopteryx)
7 A horse (horse)
8 Classes (phylum)
9 1 (dog)
10 A crustacean (barnacle)

113   Asia

1 Assisted by wind (sea transport – panel)
2 Indonesia (Indonesia – panel)
3 Bahrain (Bahrain)
4 Wind of the gods (kamikaze)
5 Iran (Isfahan)
6 Jumna (Jumna)
7 Porcelain (kakiemon)
8 Vietnam (Vietnam – panel)
9 Sanskrit (Sanskrit)
10 Laos (Laos)

114   Human Body

1 Corpus luteum (progesterone)
2 Heart (heart)
3 Luteinizing hormone (luteinizing hormone)
4 Neck (human body)
5 Spleen (spleen)
6 Hypothalamus (hypothalamus)
7 Pancreas (pancreas)
8 c) 206 (bone)
9 Adrenal (corticosteroid)
10 Liver (urea)

115   Comedians and Clowns

1 Fatty Arbuckle (Arbuckle)
2 Max Wall (Wall)
3 *New Yorker* (Addams)
4 Ben Travers (Travers)
5 James Thurber (Thurber)
6 Mack Sennett (Sennett)
7 *Punch* (*Punch*)
8 Doonesbury (comic strip)
9 Harpo (Marx Brothers)
10 Roadrunner (roadrunner)

116   Solar System

1 3 (Saturn)
2 Earth (Earth)
3 1958 (Pioneer probes)
4 *Apollo 7* (Apollo project)
5 Neptune (Neptune)
6 Jupiter (Jupiter)
7 Methane (Neptune)
8 William Herschel (Herschel)
9 Helium (Jupiter)
10 *Apollo 17* (Apollo project)

117   Literature

1 *The Last Tycoon* (Fitzgerald)
2 *the Matter* (Greene)
3 Ovid (Ovid)
4 *Gloucester* (Potter)
5 Father and son (Rabelais)
6 Samuel Taylor Coleridge (Coleridge)
7 Patrick White (White)
8 Edgar Allan Poe (Poe)
9 Pushkin (Pushkin)
10 *Prima Donna* (Ionesco)

118   Sports and Games

1 26 miles 385 yards (marathon)
2 Johannesburg (cricket)
3 Snatch and jerk (weightlifting)
4 Yachts (yachting)
5 India (chess)
6 Roller skating (skating)
7 Graham Gooch (Gooch)
8 He refused to join the US army (Ali)
9 Volleyball (volleyball)
10 St Leger (horse racing)

1. 6 (quark)
2. 3 (quark)
3. Positron (positron)
4. Neutron (neutron)
5. Electron (electron)
6. Lepton (lepton)
7. Neutrino (neutrino)
8. Quarks (quark)
9. Ernest Rutherford (Rutherford)
10. Proton (proton)

1. The polar skies (aurora)
2. Gastroliths (gastrolith)
3. The ionosphere (atmosphere)
4. Chlorine (chlorofluorocarbon)
5. Aquifers (aquifer)
6. Radon (radon)
7. In igneous rock (intrusion)
8. A soil scientist (podzol)
9. Obsidian (obsidian)
10. Carrara (Carrara)

1. Ballet (Ashton)
2. Existentialism (Camus)
3. Nepal (Buddha)
4. Luke (Luke)
5. Oberon (Oberon)
6. Aikido (aikido)
7. Pierre Cardin (Cardin)
8. Hardness of minerals (Mohs' scale)
9. Iceland (parliament)
10. Molière (Molière)

1. Jørn Utzon (Australian architecture)
2. Robert O'Hara Burke and William Wills (Burke)
3. Germaine Greer (Greer, Germaine)
4. Murray (Murray)
5. Capt William Bligh (Bligh)
6. Lake Dumbleyung (Campbell, Donald)
7. Perth (America's Cup)
8. *Schindler's Ark* (Keneally)
9. Amelia Earhart (Earhart)
10. South Australia and Victoria (Australia)

1. Glass (Tiffany)
2. A mycoprotein (Quorn)
3. Iron oxide (rust)
4. Swedish (tungsten)
5. Ketone (camphor)
6. Ammonia (Haber process)
7. Cytoplasm (cytoplasm)
8. Gold (florin)
9. Basalt (Rosetta stone)
10. Bakelite (Bakelite)

124   Europe

1 Byron (Byron)
2 Finland (Finland – panel)
3 Third Crusade (crusade)
4 Fjords (Norway – panel)
5 Vltava (Prague)
6 Eagle (Albania – panel)
7 Luxembourg (Luxembourg)
8 Portuguese (Camoëns)
9 *Calypso* (Cousteau)
10 Náxos (Náxos)

125   Technology

1 Duck (wave power)
2 Priest (Stirling engine)
3 Wing (aeroplane)
4 1956 (telecommunications)
5 Nylon (synthetic)
6 Casting (moulding)
7 Carbon dioxide (fermentation)
8 Ultrasound (ultrasound scanning)
9 Steam engine (engine)
10 Coil (ignition coil)

126   Murders and Assassinations

1 Rasputin (Rasputin)
2 Michael Collins (Collins)
3 Dr Crippen (Crippen)
4 Spencer Perceval (Perceval)
5 James Garfield (Garfield)
6 Malcolm X (Malcolm X)
7 Edward the Martyr (Edward the Martyr)
8 In the Senate house (Caesar)
9 Charles Lindbergh (Lindbergh – caption)
10 St Bartholomew's Day (St Bartholomew, Massacre of)

127   Politics

1 Kate Millett (Millett)
2 Marquess (marquess)
3 Pakistan People's Party (Bhutto)
4 Opposing Québec separatism (Trudeau, Pierre)
5 *The North Briton* (Wilkes)
6 Gough Whitlam (Whitlam)
7 Lady Falkender (Falkender)
8 Harry S Truman (Fair Deal)
9 1991 (Gorbachev)
10 King Idris (Khaddhafi)

128   Genes

1 Chromosomes (gene)
2 Messenger RNA (gene shears)
3 Ribosomes (ribosome)
4 Locus (chromosome)
5 Codon (codon)
6 Guanine (DNA – caption)
7 X chromosome (sex linkage)
8 Phosphate (DNA – caption)
9 Cystic fibrosis (gene therapy)
10 Thymine (DNA – caption)

129   Visual Arts

1 Degas (Degas)
2 Inigo Jones (Jones)
3 Yosemite (Adams – caption)
4 Rubens (Rubens)
5 Tintoretto (Tintoretto)
6 Henry Moore (Moore)
7 CAD (CAD)
8 Brussels (Brussels – picture)
9 Winnie-the-Pooh stories (*Winnie-the-Pooh*)
10 Christo (Christo)

130   Quote, Unquote

1   Laurence Oates (Oates – quote)
2   A house (Le Corbusier – quote)
3   The Panama Canal (Panama Canal – quote)
4   Life (life – quote)
5   Oscar Wilde (Wilde – quote)
6   Advertising (McLuhan – quote)
7   Desperation (Thoreau – quote)
8   Abraham Lincoln (Lincoln – quote)
9   Magna Carta (Magna Carta – quote)
10   Existentialism (existentialism – quote)

131   General Knowledge

1   Thomas Gainsborough (Gainsborough)
2   Athena (Athena)
3   Milan (Mussolini)
4   Kirk Douglas (Douglas, Kirk)
5   Corinthian (order)
6   Cathedral (cathedral)
7   Vita Sackville-West (Sackville-West)
8   A bird (frogmouth)
9   Amsterdam (Amsterdam)
10   Richard Trevithick (Trevithick)

132   Elements

1   A metalloid (metalloid)
2   Iodine (iodine)
3   Magnesium (magnesium)
4   Nitrogen (amino acid)
5   Osmium (osmium)
6   Calcium (calcium)
7   Caesium (caesium)
8   Calcium (fluorite)
9   12 (periodic table)
10   Uranium (pitchblende)

133   North America

1   Labrador (Newfoundland)
2   Liberty Island (New York)
3   Harrison (Harrison)
4   San Antonio (Alamo, the)
5   Montezuma II (Mexico)
6   Delaware (Delaware)
7   Continental Congress (Continental Congress)
8   Mount McKinley (Rocky Mountains)
9   Irving Berlin (Berlin)
10   Detroit (Motown)

134   Medicine and Health

1   Aspirin (aspirin)
2   Menopause (hormone-replacement therapy)
3   Kidney (diabetes)
4   Smallpox (smallpox)
5   Salivary glands (malaria – caption)
6   Brain (dopamine)
7   Obstetrics (amniocentesis)
8   Cancer (Hodgkin's disease)
9   Thymus (T cell)
10   Tuberculosis (Lawrence)

135   Beliefs and Ideas

1   Taoism (Taoism)
2   Liberation theology (liberation theology)
3   Diggers (Diggers)
4   Sikhism (Sikhism)
5   Trotsky (Trotsky)
6   Ignatius Loyola (Ignatius Loyola)
7   Shrine (Kaaba)
8   Salvation Army (Salvation Army)
9   Aramaic (Aramaic language)
10   Johann Kepler (Kepler)

136   Universe

1 Martin Ryle (Ryle)
2 Doppler effect (red shift)
3 A nebula (nebula)
4 A unit of distance (parsec)
5 Albert Einstein (ether)
6 Ten (superstring theory)
7 Pulsar (pulsar)
8 Steady-state theory (steady-state theory)
9 Spiral (galaxy)
10 Fusion (Sun)

137   Film and TV

1 John Barrymore (Barrymore)
2 Bengal (Ray)
3 Peter Weir (Weir)
4 Roald Dahl (Dahl)
5 Hilversum (Hilversum)
6 Greta Garbo (Garbo – caption)
7 Lillian Gish (Gish)
8 *Klute* (Fonda)
9 Arthur Miller (Miller)
8 Goldfish (Goldwyn)

138   Music

1 Marimba (marimba)
2 Cremona (Stradivari)
3 *Parsifal* (Wagner)
4 Dublin (Handel)
5 John Philip Sousa (Sousa; sousaphone)
6 Folk songs and dances (Sharp)
7 Harrison Birtwistle (Birtwistle)
8 Metronome (metronome)
9 Camille Saint-Saëns (Saint-Saëns)
10 Hymns (Wesley)

139 Reflections in Science

1 James Hutton (uniformitarianism)
2 William of Occam (Occam)
3 Thomas Kuhn (Kuhn)
4 Fritz Haber (Haber)
5 Empiricism (empiricism)
6 Logical positivism (positivism)
7 C P Snow (Snow)
8 Paul Feyerabend (Feyerabend)
9 Robert Oppenheimer (Oppenheimer – quote)
10 The problem of induction (induction)

140   On the Stage

1 *A Long Day's Journey into Night* (O'Neill)
2 Richard Burbage (Burbage)
3 Dustin Hoffman (Hoffman)
4 Lawrence of Arabia (Rattigan)
5 Dionysus (theatre)
6 Louis XIV (Molière)
7 Kurt Weill (Brecht)
8 Architecture (Vanbrugh)
9 Alec Douglas-Home (Douglas-Home)
10 Antonio (*Merchant of Venice, The*)

141   Built World

1 Shah Jahan (Taj Mahal)
2 Nicholas Hawksmoor (Hawksmoor)
3 Les Invalides (Paris)
4 Guggenheim Museum (Wright)
5 Seville (Milan – picture)
6 Pakistan and China (Karakoram Highway)
7 Arizona (BioSphere 2)
8 Holyrood House (Edinburgh)
9 The prison (Venice)
10 Zambezi (Zambezi)

142   Environment

1 Union Carbide (Bhopal)
2 Methane (methane)
3 OPEC (Organization of Petroleum-Exporting Countries)
4 A virus (myxomatosis)
5 A kind of zebra (quagga)
6 St Francis of Assisi (Francis of Assisi)
7 Rubber tappers (Mendes)
8 Oryx leucoryx (oryx)
9 Alaska (Exxon Corporation)
10 Dibromoethane (petrol)

143   Who, What, Where?

1 Elizabeth Garrett Anderson (Anderson)
2 Wounded Knee (Wounded Knee)
3 An island (Bora-Bora)
4 Paul McCartney (McCartney)
5 Romansch (Switzerland – panel)
6 Ujiji (Stanley)
7 Erasmus (Erasmus)
8 Cagliari (Cagliari)
9 Paris (Crimean War; Paris, Treaty of)
10 Holman Hunt (Hunt)

144   Latin America and the Caribbean

1 Santo Domingo (Santo Domingo)
2 Uruguay (Tupamaros)
3 Bajan (Barbados – panel)
4 Salvador Allende (Allende)
5 Aconcagua (Aconcagua)
6 Brazilian (Villa-Lobos)
7 El Salvador and Honduras (El Salvador – panel)
8 Spanish and Quechna (Peru – panel)
9 White (Argentina – panel)
10 Destroyer of boats (Amazon)

145   Plant Kingdom

1   Sporophyte (fern; sporophyte)
2   Light reaction (photosynthesis)
3   Perfume (bergamot)
4   Rafflesia arnoldiana (rafflesia)
5   Mandrake (Machiavelli)
6   Bach (Bach flower healing)
7   Phloem (aphid)
8   Fungus (rust)
9   Yew (yew)
10   Narcissus (Narcissus)

146   Cats and Dogs

1   Luchino Visconti (Visconti)
2   Frederick Forsyth (Forsyth)
3   Felix the Cat (Felix the Cat)
4   Suffragettes (Cat and Mouse Act)
5   W H Auden (Auden)
6   Volkswagen (Wolfsburg)
7   Haile Selassie (Haile Selassie)
8   Miniature (poodle)
9   Dachshund (dachshund)
10   Miles Davis (Davis)

147   History

1   Aneurin Bevan (Bevan)
2   War of Spanish Succession (Ramillies, Battle of)
3   Visigoths (Alaric)
4   Robespierre (Robespierre)
5   Valley Forge (Valley Forge)
6   Switzerland (Habsburg)
7   Martin Luther (Luther)
8   Culloden (Culloden)
9   Hermann Goering (Goering)
10   Salvador Allende (Chile)

148   Myth and Magic

1   Apollo (Artemis)
2   Aleister Crowley (Crowley)
3   Charles Perrault (Perrault)
4   Thomas Malory (Malory)
5   Graces (Graces)
6   Salem (Salem)
7   May 1 (Walpurga, St)
8   Dennis Wheatley (Wheatley)
9   Leda (Leda)
10   Babylonian (Marduk)

149   People

1   Berber (Berber)
2   Héloïse (Abelard)
3   Earl Marshal (Earl Marshal)
4   Adlai Stevenson (Stevenson)
5   Photography (Avedon)
6   Photography (Carroll)
7   New York (Callas)
8   Gabrielle (Chanel)
9   La Pasionaria (Ibarruri)
10   Thomas Malthus (Malthus)

150   On Wheels

1   Sulky (horse racing)
2   Jaguar (Jaguar)
3   J B Dunlop (bicycle)
4   New York (tramway)
5   Model F (Ford – picture)
6   Stockton and Darlington (railway)
7   Hesketh (Hunt)
8   France (car)
9   Mitsubishi (car: chronology – panel)
10   Hispano Suiza (Bugatti)